Timea Havar-Simonovich,
Daniel Simonovich
(eds.)

Contemporary Theory and Practice of Organizations

Part II: Leading and Changing
the Organization

Timea Havar-Simonovich,
Daniel Simonovich
(eds.)

CONTEMPORARY THEORY AND PRACTICE OF ORGANIZATIONS

Part I: Leading and Changing
the Organization

ibidem-Verlag
Stuttgart

Bibliografische Information der Deutschen Nationalbibliothek
Die Deutsche Nationalbibliothek verzeichnet diese Publikation in der Deutschen Nationalbibliografie; detaillierte bibliografische Daten sind im Internet über http://dnb.d-nb.de abrufbar.

Bibliographic information published by the Deutsche Nationalbibliothek
Die Deutsche Nationalbibliothek lists this publication in the Deutsche Nationalbibliografie; detailed bibliographic data are available in the Internet at http://dnb.d-nb.de.

∞

Gedruckt auf alterungsbeständigem, säurefreien Papier
Printed on acid-free paper

ISBN: 978-3-8382-0748-3

© *ibidem*-Verlag
Stuttgart 2016

Alle Rechte vorbehalten

Das Werk einschließlich aller seiner Teile ist urheberrechtlich geschützt. Jede Verwertung außerhalb der engen Grenzen des Urheberrechtsgesetzes ist ohne Zustimmung des Verlages unzulässig und strafbar. Dies gilt insbesondere für Vervielfältigungen, Übersetzungen, Mikroverfilmungen und elektronische Speicherformen sowie die Einspeicherung und Verarbeitung in elektronischen Systemen.

All rights reserved. No part of this publication may be reproduced, stored in or introduced into a retrieval system, or transmitted, in any form, or by any means (electronical, mechanical, photocopying, recording or otherwise) without the prior written permission of the publisher. Any person who does any unauthorized act in relation to this publication may be liable to criminal prosecution and civil claims for damages.

Printed in the EU

Contents

Introduction 7

Section I: Leadership 9

Authentic Leadership 11
    Melanie Schmid, Timea Havar-Simonovich

Charismatic Leadership 25
    Jonathan Kappler, Thomas Schmidt

Humble Leadership 39
    Katharina Sophie Vorwig, Felix Weichsel

Section II: Coaching 53

Leadership Coaching 55
    Simon Knoll, Cormac Stafford, Debora Benson

Executive Coaching 75
    Maren Bärenfänger, Timea Havar-Simonovich

Team Coaching 89
    Alyssa Mattwig, Anna Lena Theine, Debora Benson

Section III: Organizational Interventions 103

Organizational Consulting 105
    Corinna Horn, Lisa Molitor

Change Agents 119
    Xenia Davidoff, Patrick Bertram

Organizational Learning 133
    Daniel Dierkes, Christian Enderle

Turnaround Management 147
    Michaela Kegel, Lukas Söntgerath

Introduction

This is the second of two volumes dedicated to the state of research and practice in organizations. It is a joint effort of graduates of the Master's in International Management at ESB Business School at Reutlingen University in Germany. While the first volume is dedicated to understanding the organization, this volume focuses on leading and changing organizations. It does so by highlighting current knowledge and the need for further research in three contemporary areas of organizational leadership: modern leadership approaches, coaching practices and organizational interventions.

Dedicated to recent or re-emerging aspects leadership, the first section looks at the role of authenticity, charisma and humility in business leadership. Leaders' charisma has been studied with continuing interest, resulting in frameworks and contributions that link charismatic leadership to followers' and organizational performance. While many authors emphasize the positive nature of that link, others disagree, which lends to the need for some further research. In the absence of a universally accepted definition, authentic leadership and its effect on business performance have been subject to debate. Like authentic leadership, humble leadership has played an important role recently in leadership practice and research, while suffering from the absence of a universally accepted definition. Furthermore, humility in leaders can be viewed from different angles including cognitive, motivational and appearance-related perspectives. Thus the contribution on humble leadership highlights empirical efforts that draw on a wide range of methodological approaches.

The second section of this volume is dedicated to coaching in business, a practice that has progressed to an overwhelming presence in the corporate world. However, this popularity has not lead to according efforts in research. In fact, the literature on leadership coaching is dominated by practitioner articles that focus on best practices. The contribution on leadership coaching presented in this section presents a review of underrepresented empirical works and derives important research gaps to be filled. A further contribution in this section looks at the related topic of executive coaching and its impact on organizations, where the reviewed literature witnesses, among others, the need for accurate measurement of results. Team coaching concludes the second section of this volume.

The third and last section of this book takes on concepts and instruments relevant for organizational change. The interest in the process of planned change has created the professional role of the change agent. While research on this role arguably spans half a century, some underexplored areas are highlighted and suggestions for future research made. A domain almost neglected in research, it seems, is organizational consulting. While this subject has been influenced by more established areas, such as organizational development, many unexplored areas can be identified. By contrast, organisational learning has enjoyed academic attention and debates dating back to the 1960s. The contribution on organizational learning, and the related notion of the learning organization, provides a structured literature review and turns the attention to the concept's breadth and ambiguity. Turnaround management, the systematic and rapid implementation of a range of measures to correct a seriously unprofitable situation, concludes the section on organizational interventions. Research on this practice-inspired topic is screened and discussed with emphasis on root causes of decline, the turnaround process and promising management approaches.

Overall, this volume brings together ten contemporary topics relevant for leading and changing today's organizations, while showing to what extent research efforts have achieved to supply substantiated knowledge and guidance.

Section I: Leadership

Authentic Leadership

Melanie Schmid, Timea Havar-Simonovich

Abstract. The concept of an authentic leader is not new and has been explored throughout history. However, based on the holistic discussion of authentic leadership it can be concluded that there is no universally accepted approach towards a definition of authentic leadership and – more importantly – how to achieve authentic leadership. Therefore, the topic of authentic leadership is controversially discussed, as outlined in this article. Based on this review the approach of centering authentic leadership on authenticity and identification seems most plausible. Nonetheless, many authors in the research literature also emphasize the coherence of identification, authenticity, emotions, trust and values. In linking authentic leadership to positive organizational behavior, some researchers believe that a better performance can be achieved in an organization if leadership is based on authenticity and trust.

Keywords: Authentic leadership, leadership, leadership theory, authenticity, international management, trust, motivation, theoretical leadership frameworks, positive organizational behavior

1 Introduction

For the past decades, scholars have sometimes tried to develop the perfect leadership model (George et al., 2007). However, until now no best practice model has been developed. Starbucks CEO Howard Schultz said in his interview with Ignatius (2010) about the mastering of the company's crisis with regards to a good leader:

> *"You have to be honest and authentic and not hide. I think the leader today has to demonstrate both transparency and vulnerability, and with that comes truthfulness and humility and obviously the ability to instill confidence in people, and not through some top-down hierarchical approach (p. 5)."*

The idea of an authentic leader is not new and has been explored throughout history (Kruse 2013). But only after the publishing of Bill George's book *Authentic Leadership* in 2003, the topic has drawn the increased attention of researchers (George et al. 2007). Therefore, the aim of this article is to examine the research conducted on Authentic Leadership (AL) after 2003 in a holistic approach, to highlight some advancement in the field and potential disagreements among scholars.

Firstly, AL is defined and frameworks are introduced, as can be seen in Figure 1. Secondly, major literature published on AL after 2003 is clustered into different approaches theoretical strands. Thirdly, critical voices and potential challenges towards AL are highlighted and future study fields and research gaps are presented. Finally, a critical review and an outlook finalize this article on AL.

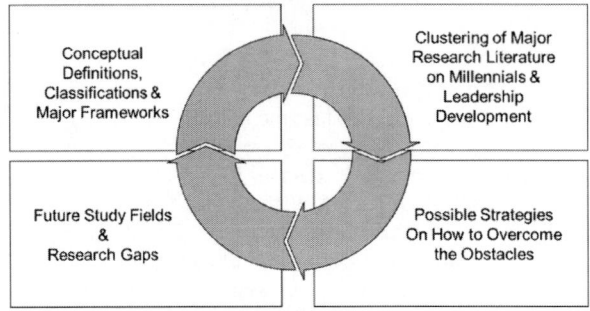

Figure 1: Structure of this article on AL

2 Conceptual Foundation and Definitions of AL

In the following chapter, a first approach to defining AL is made and subsequently major frameworks and models are introduced.

2.1 Approach to Defining Authentic Leadership

Until now researchers could not agree on a single definition of AL. Ilies et al. (2005) have defined authentic leaders as individuals who are

> *"deeply aware of their values and beliefs, they are self-confident, genuine, reliable and trustworthy, and they focus on building followers' strengths, broadening their thinking and creating a positive and engaging organizational context (p. 374)."*

Shamir & Eilam (2005), who support the idea of AL emerging from the person's life story, based their definition on the individual's self-concept and self-awareness. The authors state that the person's self-knowledge is derived from the life story because it can provide the leadership with an underlying meaning and identity (Kegan 1983). Avolio et al. (2004) also believe that individuals can develop AL through self-awareness. However, the authors build AL on positive organizational behavior (POB), development of trust and identification. To draw a conclusion based on the different approaches as will be highlighted in chapter 3, there is no universal definition on AL. [?]

2.2 AL Models & Frameworks

In 2005, Gardner et al. (2005) established an AL development model, which was based on the theoretical foundation of identity research, as illustrated in Figure 2 (Hoyle et al. 1999; Leary & Tangney 2003).

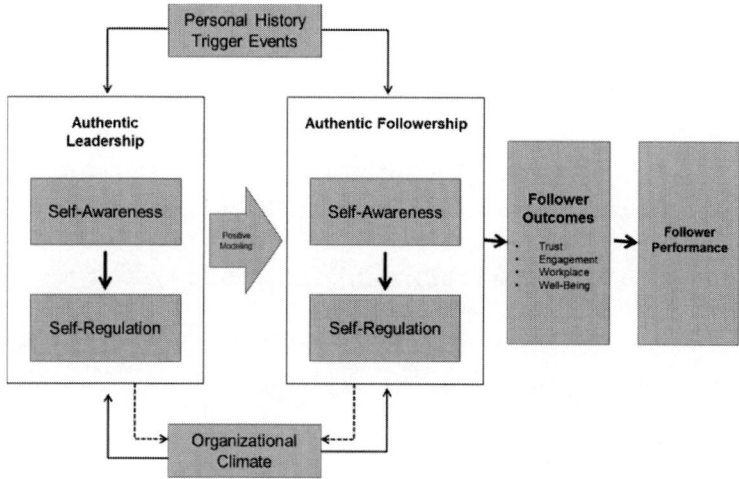

Figure 2: The Conceptual Framework for Authentic Leader and Follower Development (Source: Gardner et al. 2005)

Consistent with Shamir & Eilam (2005), the authors view the leader's life story as the antecedent of AL development. In accordance with the views of Luthans & Avolio (2003), Gardner et al. (2005) regard self-awareness as the foundation of AL. Eagly (2005) complements this approach and argues that good leaders must not only act on their values but also strive for the agreement and sharing of the leader's values by the followers. Only under these circumstances can a leader create identification, which increases the organization's success because, in accordance with Gardner et al. (2005), leadership resides in leader's actions as well as in the follower's reactions. Eagly (2005) claims in her research that for outsider groups in general, and female leaders in particular, it is more challenging to gain a high level of leader-instilled identification than for men.

Ilies et al. (2005) developed a further model (see Figure 3), which complements previous concepts and processes (Avolio & Gardner 2005; Gardner et al. 2005; Luthans & Avolio 2003; May et al. 2003). The authors propose that future research should focus also more on the effects of follower's eudemonic well-being.

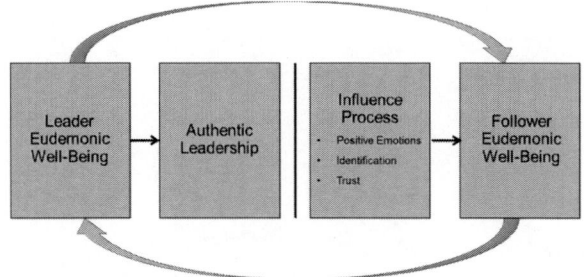

Figure 3: The Influence of AL on the Eudemonic Well-Being (Source: Ilies et al. 2005)

3 Literature on Authentic Leadership

In this chapter, the existing research literature is clustered in different approaches towards AL. This also includes criticism, challenges and research gaps.

3.1 Clustering of the Literature

On the basis of the research papers of the authors Gardner et al. (2011), Novicevic et al. (2006), Avolio & Gardner (2005) and Avolio et al. (2009), this review distinguishes between different aspects of AL. The main research contributions, which form the basis of this review, are listed in Appendix 1. However, due to the broad range of topics within the AL theory, the clustering of literature offered in this article includes a mere selection of influential approaches and does not claim any completeness.

With regards to the previously outlined frameworks of AL, it is important to note that many of these frameworks have identified authenticity and identity as the foundation of AL. As Luthans & Avolio (2003) express, one of the leader's main challenges is the identification of the followers' strengths and to develop these to yield an optimal organizational outcome. Avolio et al. (2004) believe that the influence of AL on the followers' behavior is more powerful when they identify with their leader and share common goals (Snyder et al. 2000; Avolio et al. 2004). Furthermore, it is critical to develop trust between leaders and followers in order to enhance the identification with the leader and thus the overall performance within the organization (Avolio et al. 2004; Dirks & Ferrin 2002; Novicevic et al. 2005). Evidence for this view was provided in empirical studies conducted by Opatokun et al. (2013) and Erkutlu & Chafra (2013). Another perspective on authenticity is provided by Sparrowe (2005), who believes that AL is based on the narrative self and who bases his concept on the framework of Ricoeur (1992).

Harvey et al. (2006) have developed yet another model, which bases AL on attributions and suggests that by creating awareness in leaders for factors that might produce wrong attributions, the performance of the leader and the organization in general can be enhanced as can be seen in Figure 4. In his study, Fields (2007) observed that behaviors, which are inconsistent with the followers' view of ideal leadership, have a negative impact on the leader's authenticity and integrity. Moreover, as Cha & Edmondson (2006) highlight, explicit statements of the leader might make the follower's expectat that their leader will behave in a way that is not only consistent with the leader's values, but also with aspects beyond the leader's explicit statements.. This approach towards AL's attribution theory is supported by empirical studies of Peus et al. (2012) and Nichols & Erakovich (2013).

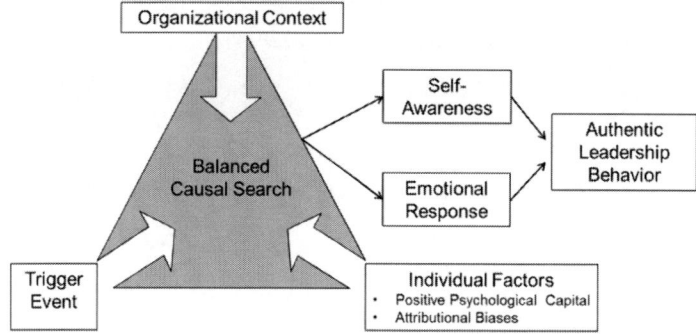

Figure 4: Attribution Model of AL (Source: Harvey et al. 2006)

In addition to authenticity and identity, many scholars regard affective processes as a foundation of AL. In 2009, Gardner et al. (2009) developed a leadership model of emotional displays, as illustrated in Figure 5.

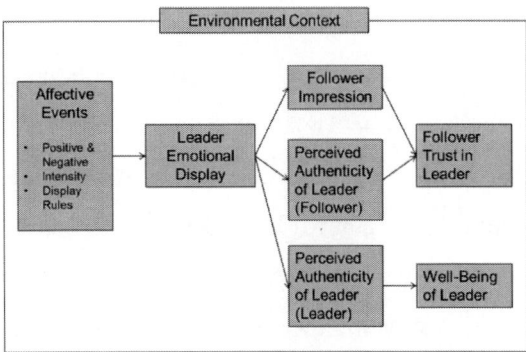

Figure 5: Leader Emotional Labor and Authenticity Model (Source: Gardner et al. 2009)

The model suggests that if the leader shows emotions, this can have a high impact on the followers. However, the authors describe the leader's dilemma of acting in an authentic way while at the same time to expressing a wide range of emotions depending on a specific context. Here Gardner et al. (2009) point to some evidence suggesting that leaders who are not necessarily authentic may very well be perceived as highly effective, as long as they show a high level of emotional intelligence. Avolio et al. (2004) support this view and stress that authentic leaders are more likely to create positive feelings and identification among followers when showing emotions. In fact, Michie & Gooty (2005) suggest that positive emotions motivate leaders to act according to their own values (Macik-Frey et al. 2009; Yagil & Medler-Liraz 2014).

Turning to ethics, scholars disagree on whether ethical principles should be included in the AL theory as a basic element or not. Walumbwa et al. (2008), for example, have included the moral perspective as a foundational element in their AL theory and Ladkin & Taylor (2010) have associated AL with moral leadership in their papers, too (Ambrose et al. 2008). With regards to the ethical approach of AL, Zhu et al. (2011) developed a theoretical model, which illustrates the impact of AL on the followers' ethical decision-making (see Figure 6). This model is also empirically supported by studies from Hannah et al. (2011) and May et al. (2003) who associate AL positively to the follower's display of moral courage.

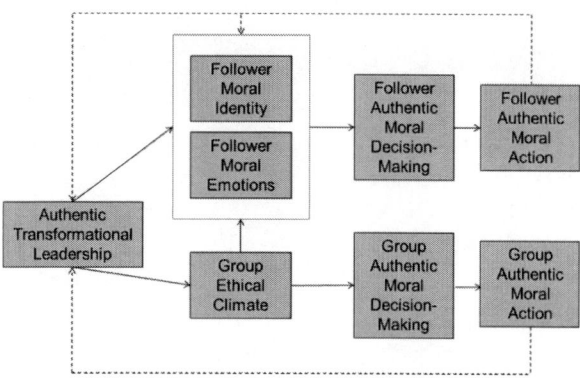

Figure 6: The Impact of AL on Follower's Ethical Decision-Making Model (Source: Zhu et al. 2011)

Another AL direction emphasizes AL's impact on happiness and well-being. Jensen & Luthans (2006) have built on other AL models of (Avolio et al. 2004; Avolio & Luthans 2006; Luthans & Avolio 2003) in their study and their results show a positive impact of AL on the follower's attitudes and level of happiness. Quite a few authors, including Gardner et al. (2005), Ilies et al. (2005), Shamir & Eilam (2005), Gardner et al. (2009), Macik-Frey et al. (2009), Walumbwa et al. (2010) and Wong & Cummings (2009) all regard the well-being and engagement of the leader with the followers as important outcomes. The empirical study of Walumbwa et al. (2010) provides further evidence for this relationship (Gardner et al. 2005; Ilies et al. 2005; Shamir & Eilam 2005). Alok & Israel's (2012) study shows that AL can positively impact the followers' work commitment when followers feel that their leaders personally express the organizational mission. In line with Gardner et al. (2005), this study concludes that authentic leaders can create a more caring, engaged and development-oriented culture in organizations (Leroy et al. 2012; Toor & Ofori 2009; Nielsen et al. 2013).

Yammarino et al. (2008) have integrated AL and positive organizational behavior (POB) in their framework and believe that by developing AL, the organization's behavior is positively influenced, thereby enhancing the outcome of the organization (see Figure 7). In fact, the authors regard AL as the connection between POB and the overall performance of the organization.

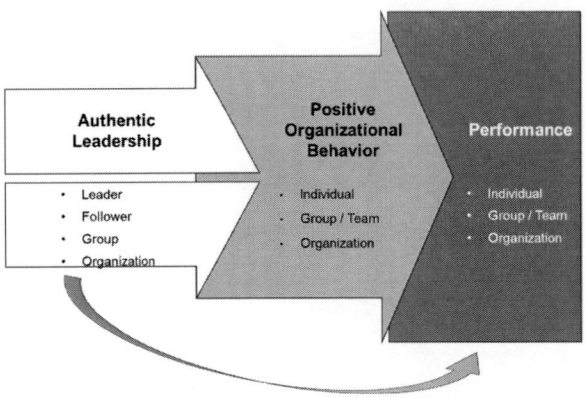

Figure 7: Positive Organizational Behavior and AL (Yammarino et al. 2008)

In support of this framework, it should not go unmentioned that the framework of Luthans & Avolio (2003) originally also included POB. Furthermore, Avolio & Gardner (2005) agree in their research paper that there is a significant relationship between AL and POB even though they regard the two to be distinctive from each other. In addition, Jensen & Luthans (2006), Macik-Frey et al. (2009), Wong & Cummings (2009) and Yammarino et al. (2008) all regard POB as an important foundation of AL. Walumbwa et al. (2010) found out in their empirical study that AL behavior was "positively related to supervisor-rated organizational citizenship behavior and work engagement, controlling for ideal power distance, company type, and followers' demographics such as age and sex" (p. 901). The authors further suggest that the follower's identification with the leader is critical for his performance (Hmieleski et al. 2012; Peterson et al. 2012; Hsiung 2012; Rego et al. 2014; Müceldili et al. 2013; model of Jones & Crompton 2009).

A few authors also focus their AL research on the influence of transformational leadership (TL) theories on AL. Luthans & Avolio (2003), for example, regard the influence of TL on AL as rather high. Avolio & Gardner (2005) view AL as the foundation, which can combine aspects of charismatic, spiritual and transformational leadership. In addition Walumbwa et al. (2008) claim in their empirical work that AL is influenced by more measures than transformational and ethical leadership.

3.2 Criticism and Challenges of AL

Diddams & Chang (2012) point out that so far little research has been done on what role weaknesses play in AL. The authors argue that weaknesses are not a separate characteristic and should therefore be included in current AL development models and measurements (Walumbwa et al. 2008). Following this critique, Costas & Taheri (2012) feel that due to the fact that AL emphasizes positive emotions only, little room is left for 'negative' emotions (Ford & Harding 2011). Algera & Lips-Wiersma (2012) put forward that AL provokes unrealistic anticipations by not acknowledging the natural existence of inauthenticity in organizations. In addition, they believe that it is impractical to build AL on commonly shared values and goals, since in many organizations these are likely to be divergent (Algera & Lips-Wiersma 2012; Hewlin 2003). Moreover, Algera & Lips-Wiersma (2012) propound that AL can create false moral confidence in leaders and followers by creating the assumption that authenticity automatically leads to an ethical behavior. Finally, Endrissat et al. (2007) believe that authentic leaders are constantly faced with a real challenge of fulfilling the tasks and at the same time maintaining personal relationships (Harter 2002).

3.3 Need for further study

So far the majority of research conducted on AL is conceptual. Therefore Gardner et al. (2011) suggest that in the future more theory generating research should be done. Nichols & Erakovich (2013) identified gaps between theoretical work and empirical evidence and suggest that more empirical investigations with representative samples should be undertaken. Furthermore, specific measurements of AL need to be developed to provide evidence for the established AL theories (Avolio et al. 2009). In addition, Nichols & Erakovich (2013) constituted a need for more clarity in how AL is regarded across different cultures and situations and whether it can be seen as a universally applicable theoretical construct or not. Also, attention to authentic followership and AL development should be emphasized more (Gardner et al. 2011).

4 Summary

This article has outlined different approaches towards AL. In summary, it can be stated that there is no universal agreement on how AL is defined and thus how to obtain it. Consequently, AL remains subject to controversial discussions and it will be interesting to see how the research field will develop in the future. So far, it can be stated that, based on the amount of published research papers, the approach of centering AL on authenticity and identification seems most common. However, due to the fact that authenticity, identification, trust, emotions and values are all related domains, it is not surprising that many scholars also emphasize them, too. In particular, the link between AL and POB is close and one could argue that many scholars in the end believe that authenticity can be a driver for better corporate performance.

Appendix

Appendix 1: Clustering of Major Literature on AL

Theoretical Frameworks	(Luthans & Avolio, 2003); (May et al., 2003); (Avolio et al., 2004); (Avolio & Gardner, 2005); (Ilies et al., 2005); (Shamir & Eilam, 2005); (Avolio & Luthans, 2006); (Walumbwa et al., 2008)
Authenticity & Identity	(Leary & Tangney, 2003); (Luthans & Avolio, 2003); (Avolio et al., 2004); (Gardner et al., 2005); (Ilies et al., 2005); (Shamir & Eilam, 2005); (Sparrowe, 2005)
Attribution Theory, Theories of Social & Leader Perception	(Harvey et al., 2006); (Fields, 2007)
Affective Processes & Ethical and Value-Based Leadership	(Avolio & Gardner, 2005); (Michie & Gooty, 2005); (Ambrose et al., 2008); (Gardner et al., 2009); (Walumbwa et al., 2010); (Ladkin & Taylor, 2010)
Well-Being, Vital Engagement	(Gardner et al., 2005); (Ilies et al., 2005); (Shamir & Eilam, 2005); (Gardner et al., 2009); (Macik-Frey et al., 2009); (Wong & Cummings, 2009); (Walumbwa et al., 2010)
Positive Organizational Behavior	(Luthans, 2002); (Luthans & Avolio, 2003); (Avolio & Gardner, 2005); (Jensen & Luthans, 2006); (Yammarino et al., 2008); (Macik-Frey et al., 2009); (Wong & Cummings, 2009)
Theories of Charismatic, Transformational, Visionary Leadership	(Luthans & Avolio, 2003); (Avolio & Gardner, 2005); (Walumbwa et al., 2008)

References

Algera, P. M. & Lips-Wiersma, M., 2012. Radical Authentic Leadership: Co-creating the conditions under which all members of the organization can be authentic. *The Leadership Quarterly,* Volume 23, pp. 118-131.

Alok, K. & Israel, D., 2012. Authentic Leadership & Work Engagement. *The Indian Journal of Industrial Relations,* 47(3), pp. 498-510.

Ambrose, M. L., Arnaud, A. & Schminke, M., 2008. Individual Moral Development and Ethical Climate: The Influence of Person–Organization Fit on Job Attitudes. *Journal of Business Ethics,* Volume 77, p. 323–333.

Avolio, B. J. & Gardner, W. L., 2005. Authentic leadership development: Getting to the root of positive forms of leadership. *The Leadership Quarterly,* Volume 16, p. 315–338.

Avolio, B. J. et al., 2004. Unlocking the mask: A look at the process by which authentic leaders' impact follower attitudes and behaviors. *The Leadership Quarterly,* Volume 15, p. 801–823.

Avolio, B. J. & Luthans, F., 2006. *The High Impact Leader: Moments Matter in Accelerating Authentic Leadership Development.* New York, NY: McGraw-Hill.

Avolio, B. J., Walumbwa, F. O. & Weber, T. J., 2009. Leadership: Current Theories, Research, and Future Directions. *Annual Review of Psychology,* Volume 60, pp. 421-449.

Cha, S. & Edmondson, A., 2006. When values backfire: Leadership, attribution, and disenchantment in a values-driven organization. *The Leadership Quarterly,* Volume 17, p. 57–78.

Cooper, C. D., Scandura, T. A. & Schriesheim, C. A., 2005. Looking forward but learning from our past: Potential challenges to developing authentic leadership theory and authentic leaders. *The Leadership Quarterly,* Volume 16, p. 475–493.

Costas, J. & Taheri, A., 2012. The Return of the Primal Father' in Postmodernity? A Lacanian Analysis of Authentic Leadership. *Organization Studies,* 33(9), p. 1195–1216.

Diddams, M. & Chang, G. C., 2012. Only human: Exploring the nature of weakness in authentic leadership. *The Leadership Quarterly,* Volume 23, p. 593–603.

Dirks, K. T. & Ferrin, D. L., 2002. Trust in leadership: Meta-analytic findings and implications for research and practice. *Journal of Applied Psychology,* Issue 87, pp. 611-628.

Eagly, A. H., 2005. Achieving relational authenticity in leadership: Does gender matter?. *The Leadership Quarterly,* Volume 16, p. 459–474.

Endrissat, N., Müller, W. R. & Kaudela-Baum, S., 2007. En Route to an Empirically-Based Understanding of Authentic Leadership. *European Management Journal,* 25(3), p. 207–220.

Erkutlu, H. & Chafra, J., 2013. Effects of trust and psychological contract violation on authentic leadership and organizational deviance. *Management Research Review,* 36(9), pp. 828-848.

Fields, D. L., 2007. Determinants of Follower Perceptions of a Leader's Authenticity and Integrity. *European Management Journal,* 25(3), p. 195–206.

Ford, J. & Harding, N., 2011. The impossibility of the 'true self' of authentic leadership. *Leadership,* Volume 7, p. 463–479.

Gardner, W. L. et al., 2005. Can you see the real me? A self-based model of authentic leader and follower development. *The Leadership Quarterly,* Volume 16, p. 343–372.

Gardner, W. L., Cogliser, C. C., Davis, K. M. & Dickens, M. P., 2011. Authentic leadership: A review of the literature and research agenda. *The Leadership Quarterly,* Volume 22, p. 1120–1145.

Gardner, W. L., Fischer, D. & Hunt, J. G., 2009. Emotional labor and leadership: A threat to authenticity?. *The Leadership Quarterly,* Volume 20, p. 466–482.

George, B., Sims, P., McLean, A. N. & Mayer, D., 2007. Discovering Your Authentic Leadership. *Harvard Business Review,* Volume 02, pp. 129-138.

Hannah, S. T., Avolio, B. J. & Walumbwa, F. O., 2011. Relationships between Authentic Leadership, Moral Courage, and Ethical and Pro-Social Behaviors. *Business Ethics Quarterly,* 21(4), pp. 555-578.

Harter, S., 2002. Authenticity. In: *Handbook of Positive Psychology.* Oxford: University Press Oxford, pp. 382-394.

Harvey, P., Martinko, M. J. & Gardner, W. L., 2006. Promoting Authentic Behavior in Organizations: An Attributional Perspective. *Journal of Leadership and Organizational Studies,* 12(3), pp. 1-11.

Hewlin, P. F., 2003. And the award for best actor goes to...: Facades of conformity in organizational settings. *Academy of Management Review,* Volume 28, p. 633–642.

Hmieleski, K. M., Cole, M. S. & Baron, R. A., 2012. Shared Authentic Leadership and New Venture Performance. *Journal of Management,* 38(5), pp. 1476-1499.

Hoyle, R. H., Kernis, M. H., Leary, M. R. & Baldwin, M. W., 1999. *Selfhood: Identity, esteem, regulation.* Boulder, CO: Westview Press.

Hsiung, H.-H., 2012. Authentic Leadership and Employee Voice Behavior: A Multi-Level Psychological Process. *Journal of Business Ethics,* Volume 107, p. 349–361.

Ignatius, A., 2010. We had to Own the Mistakes: An Interview with Howard Schultz. *The Harvard Business Journal,* Volume 07, pp. 1-7.

Ilies, R., Morgeson, F. P. & Nahrgang, J. D., 2005. Authentic leadership and eudemonic well-being: Understanding leader–follower outcomes. *The Leadership Quarterly,* Volume 16, p. 373–394.

Jensen, S. M. & Luthans, F., 2006. Entrepreneurs as authentic leaders: impact on employees' attitudes. *Leadership & Organization Development Journal,* 27(8), pp. 646-666.

Jones, O. & Crompton, H., 2009. Enterprise logic and small firms: a model of authentic entrepreneurial leadership. *Journal of Strategy and Management,* 2(4), pp. 329-351.

Kegan, R., 1983. *The Evolving Self: Problem and Process in Human Development.* Cambridge, MA: Harvard University Press.

Kruse, K., 2013. *Forbes: Leadership: What is Authentic Leadership?.* [Online] Available at: http://www.forbes.com/sites/kevinkruse/2013/05/12/what-is-authentic-leadership [Accessed 15 03 2014].

Ladkin, D. & Taylor, S. S., 2010. Enacting the 'true self': Towards a theory of embodied authentic leadership. *The Leadership Quarterly,* Volume 21, p. 64–74.

Leary, M. R. & Tangney, J. P., 2003. *Handbook of self and identity.* New York: Guilford Publications.

Leroy, H., Palanski, M. E. & Simons, T., 2012. Authentic Leadership and Behavioral Integrity as Drivers of Follower Commitment and Performance. *Journal of Business Ethics,* Volume 107, p. 255–264.

Luthans, F., 2002. The need for and meaning of positive organizational behavior. *Journal of Organizational Behavior,* Volume 23, p. 695–706.

Luthans, F. & Avolio, B. J., 2003. Authentic Leadership: A Positive Development Approach. In: *Positive Organizational Scholarship.* San Francisco, CA: Berrett-Koehler, pp. 241-258.

Macik-Frey, M., Quick, J. C. & Cooper, C. L., 2009. Authentic leadership as a pathway to positive health. *Journal of Organizational Behavior,* Volume 30, p. 453–458.

May, D. R., Chan, A. Y., Hodges, T. D. & Avolio, B. J., 2003. Developing the Moral Component of Authentic Leadership. *Organizational Dynamics,* 32(3), p. 247–260.

Michie, S. & Gooty, J., 2005. Values, emotions, and authenticity: Will the real leader please stand up?. *The Leadership Quarterly,* Volume 16, p. 441–457.

Müceldili, B., Turan, H. & Erdil, O., 2013. The Influence of Authentic Leadership on Creativity and Innovativeness. *Procedia - Social and Behavioral Sciences,* Volume 99, p. 673 – 681.

Nichols, T. W. & Erakovich, R., 2013. Authentic leadership and implicit theory: a normative form of leadership?. *Leadership & Organization Development Journal,* 34(2), pp. 182-195.

Nielsen, M. B., Eid, J., Mearns, K. & Larsson, G., 2013. Authentic leadership and its relationship with risk perception and safety climate. *Leadership & Organization Development Journal,* 34(4), pp. 308-325.

Novicevic, M. M. et al., 2005. Barnard on conflicts of responsibility: Implications for today's perspectives on transformational and authentic leadership. *Management Decision,* 43(10), pp. 1396-1409.

Novicevic, M. M. et al., 2006. Authentic Leadership: A Historical Perspective. *Journal of Leadership and Organizational Studies,* 13(1), pp. 64-76.

Opatokun, K. A., Hasim, C. N. & Hassan, S. S. S., 2013. Authentic Leadership in higher learning institution: a case study of International Islamic University Malaysia (IIUM).. *International Journal of Leadership Studies,* 8(1), pp. 49-66.

Peterson, S. J., Walumbwa, F. O., Avolio, B. J. & Hannah, S. T., 2012. The relationship between authentic leadership and follower job performance: The mediating role of follower positivity in extreme contexts. *The Leadership Quarterly,* Volume 23, p. 502–516.

Peus, C. et al., 2012. Authentic Leadership: An Empirical Test of Its Antecedents, Consequences, and Mediating Mechanisms. *Journal of Business Ethics,* Volume 107, p. 331–348.

Rego, A., Sousa, F., Marques, C. & Pina e Cunha, M., 2014. Hope and positive affect mediating the authentic leadership and creativity relationship. *Journal of Business Research,* Volume 67, pp. 200-210.

Rego, A. et al., 2013. Are authentic leaders associated with more virtuous, committed and potent teams?. *The Leadership Quarterly,* Issue 24, pp. 61-79.

Ricoeur, P., 1992. *Oneself as another.* Chicago: University of Chicago Press.

Rousseau, D. M., Sitkin, S. B., Burt, R. S. & Camerer, C., 1998. Not so different after all: A cross-discipline view of trust. *Academy of Management Review,* Issue 23, pp. 393-404.

Shamir, B. & Eilam, G., 2005. What's your story? A life-stories approach to authentic leadership development. *The Leadership Quarterly,* Volume 16, p. 395–417.

Simons, T., 2002. Behavioral integrity: The perceived alignment between managers' words and deeds as a research focus. *Organization Science,* Volume 13, pp. 18-35.

Snyder, C. R. et al., 2000. The roles of hopeful thinking in preventing problems and enhancing strengths. *Applied and Preventive Psychology,* 3(15), pp. 262-295.

Snyder, C. R. et al., 1991. The will and the ways. *Journal of Personality and Social Psychology,* Issue 60, pp. 570-585.

Sparrowe, R. T., 2005. Authentic leadership and the narrative self. *The Leadership Quarterly,* Volume 16, p. 419–439.

Toor, S.-U.-R. & Ofori, G., 2009. Authenticity and its influence on psychological wellbeing and contingent self-esteem of leaders in Singapore construction sector. *Construction Management and Economics,* Volume 27, p. 299–313.

Walumbwa, F. O. et al., 2008. Authentic leadership: Development and validation of a theory-based measure. *Journal of Management,* 34(1), p. 89.

Walumbwa, F. O. et al., 2010. Psychological processes linking authentic leadership to follower behaviors. *The Leadership Quarterly,* Volume 21, p. 901–914.

Wang, H. et al., 2005. Leader–member exchange as a mediator of the relationship between transformational leadership and followers' performance and organizational citizenship behavior. *Academy of Management Journal,* 48(3), pp. 420-432.

Wong, C. A. & Cummings, G. G., 2009. The influence of authentic leadership behaviors on trust and work outcomes of health care staff. *Journal of Leadership Studies,* 3(2), pp. 6-23.

Yagil, D. & Medler-Liraz, H., 2014. Feel Free, Be Yourself: Authentic Leadership, Emotional Expression, and Employee Authenticity. *Journal of Leadership & Organizational Studies,* 21(1), p. 59–70.

Yammarino, F. J., Dionne, S. D., Schriesheim, C. A. & Dansereau, F., 2008. Authentic leadership and positive organizational behavior: A meso, multi-level perspective. *The Leadership Quarterly,* Volume 19, p. 693–707.

Zhu, W., Avolio, B. J., Riggio, R. E. & Sosik, J. J., 2011. The effect of authentic transformational leadership on follower and group ethics. *The Leadership Quarterly,* Volume 22, p. 801–817

Charismatic Leadership

Jonathan Kappler, Thomas Schmidt

Abstract. Charismatic leadership is a crucial topic in organizations that found a lot of attention over the years. The objective of this article is to provide a comprehensive review of publications and exemplary frameworks on charismatic leadership. Thereby the focus is laid on publications that examined the relationship between charismatic leadership and followers' performance and job satisfaction, as well as organizational outcomes. The findings show that most scholars clearly support that charismatic leaders positively affect followers' and organizations' performance. In fact, only very few authors disagree with the majority's opinion. On the basis of the studied articles, gaps for future research are motivated..

Keywords: Charisma, leadership, leader, teams, job satisfaction, performance

1 Introduction and structure

Over the years the concept of charismatic leadership has gained a lot of attention and an enormous body of contributions on this topic have been published. Charisma is a Greek word that can be translated as "gift" (Conger & Kanungo 1987). It was Weber (1947) who first used this term to discuss the theoretical impact of charismatic leadership on followers. He applied the concept of charismatic leadership to explain the effectiveness of a leader and revealed that this talent is based on extraordinary qualities of an individual.

The phenomenon of charisma has long been discussed in political and sociological environments to characterize leaders (House & Baetz 1979). However, in the 1980s scholars first started studying charisma in organizational settings (Bryman 1992). Two forms of charismatic leadership were distinguished: socialized and personalized leaders (e.g., Howell & Shamir 2005; Choi 2006; Howell 1988). The former reflects individuals that are non-exploitative and have the ability to motivate followers in order to maximize organizational outcomes (Choi 2006; Howell 1988). Personalized leaders, however, possess traits such as being exploitative, non-egalitarian and self-aggrandizing (Choi 2006). Conger (1989, 1990) associates this kind of leadership with the dark side of charismatic leadership.

Over the last three decades, numerous scholars published their theories about charismatic leadesrhip in an organizational context (e.g., House 1977; Shamir et al. 1993; Conger & Kanungo 1987, 1998). Especially the effects of charismatic leadership on employees and organizational outcomes have been intensely investigated (Hayibor et al. 2011). However, it can be noted that most studies were published between 1980 and 2005. After this temporal corridor, the major authors' publication activities disappeared. During the last ten years only a few research papers made valuable contributions.

Even though the range of investigated topics is large in this article literature of the following two areas will be considered only:

- Follower's performance and job satisfaction
- Organizational outcomes

The applied literature in this article primarily contains academic journals and a few books published by the major authors. In section 2 of this article first three significant exemplary studies proposed by representative scholars are demonstrated. Section 3 is the main body of this article in which views of different scholars on selected research topics are contrasted. Also this section will highlight disagreeing author's opinions. Next is to identify gaps for future research based on the review of literature (Section 4). The article closes with a conclusion summarizing what the literature says (Section 5).

2 Exemplary studies

This section briefly describes three of the most important exemplary studies in the field by House (1977), Shamir et al. (1993) and Conger and Kanungo (1987, 1998).

2.1 A psychological theory of charismatic leadership by House (1977)

House (1977) advanced the concept of charismatic leadership initiated by Weber. He was first to introduce a holistic theoretical framework of specific leader behaviors and personal traits associated with charismatic leadership analyzed from a psychological point of view. He defined charismatic leaders as those "who by force of their personal abilities are capable of having profound and extraordinary effects on followers" (House 1977, p.189). In his findings he concluded that charismatic leaders possess a high level of self-confidence and set high expectations. As a result followers consider the leader as a role model and get highly motivated to achieve exceptional performance (House 1977). House gained a lot of attention with his presented framework and probably laid the foundation for further research in an organizational context (Antonakis 2012).

2.2 A self-concept based theory by Shamir et al. (1993)

The self-concept based theory presented by Shamir et al. (1993) further developed House's concept of charismatic leadership (Yukl 2010) and focused on the motivational effects charismatic leaders have on followers in organizations. Shamir et al. (1993) proposed that charismatic leadership is mainly described on how the self-concept of followers is engaged by leaders. The main statement of their framework was that charismatic leadership is effective and has a strong positive impact on follower's motivation by increasing their self-expression, self-esteem, self-worth and self-consistency (Shamir et al. 1993).

2.3 Attribution theory of charisma by Conger and Kanungo (1987, 1998)

Conger and Kanungo (1987) offered a behavioral theory linking organizational contexts to charismatic leadership. This model explains that the concept of charisma is an attributional phenomenon and dependent on leader's behavior (Conger and Kanungo 1987, 1998). Thus, an individual can be identified as a charismatic leader through an attributional process built on follower's perception (Antonakis 2012). Conger and Kanungo (1998) introduced a three-stage process including a behavioral scale of five dimensions ("Conger Kanungo Scale") to measure charismatic leaders. This model belongs to the most utilized theories used to distinguish charismatic leadership in organizational settings nowadays (Yukl 1999).

3 Literature contributions and comparison of different author's views

This part of the article focuses on literature contributions published by the major scholars in the field of charismatic leadership and contrasts their different opinions.

3.1 Significant areas of research in the field of charismatic leadership

The publications demonstrated in this section focus on the following two topics: (1) follower's performance and job satisfaction as well as (2) organizational outcomes.

3.1.1 Publications on follower's performance and job satisfaction

Over the years many scholars explored that socialized charismatics have positive effects on their follower's performance and job satisfaction. For instance all scholars of the previous demonstrated theories (House 1977; Shamir et al. 1993; Conger & Kanungo 1987, 1998) have discussed this phenomenon and perhaps lead to the further conducted research in this field. Shamir et al. (1998) used the self-concept theory introduced by Shamir et al. (1993) as a basis for further research analyzing the impact of charismatic behavior in military units. Similarly, Yammarino et al. (1993) examined the performance of midshipmen and their subsequent leaders at the United States Naval Academy (USNA) as well as of United States Navy (USN) officers and recorded positive theoretical findings. Howell and Frost (1989) performed a laboratory study describing the interactive effects of three different leadership forms. The participants that were lead by a charismatic individual achieved better task performances and higher task adjustments. Another article published by Cicero and Pierro (2007) investigated the relationship between charismatic leadership and employee's work-group identification. The authors found positive results in terms of follower's job satisfaction and performance. Kirkpatrick and Locke (1996) stated that charismatic leadership is positively associated with follower's performance quality and quantity by conducting a laboratory simulation with students in upper-level business classes. Also Seltzer and Bass (1990) asserted that charismatic leaders have a positive influence on employees' job satisfaction under the condition of initiation and consideration of this leadership form. In a study published by Choi (2006) the impact of charismatic leadership on their follower's motivation was examined. Choi (2006) proposed that socialized charismatic leaders possess three key behavioral elements that enhance follower's needs: envisioning, empathy and empowerment. Several previous papers (e.g., Bass 1985; Burke 1986; Conger & Kanungo 1998) are in harmony with the behavioral factors suggested by Choi. Choi (2006) further summarized that these behavioral components of charismatic leaders lead to motivational effects on follower's needs such as "improved task performance, greater job satisfaction, stronger collective identity and group cohesiveness, more organizational citizenship behaviors, and stronger self-leadership among the followers" (p.24).

Most research contributions in this field focus on the positive consequences of charismatic leadership (Yukl 2010). Only a few research scholars have different sights on this topic and published theories discussing the "dark side" of charisma (e.g., Conger 1989, 1990; Conger & Kanungo 1998; Sankowsky 1995). Howell and Avolio (1992) analyzed the effects of ethical and unethical charismatic leaders on their followers in organizations. They stressed that unethical charismatic leaders "undermine followers' motivation and ability to challenge existing views, to engage in self-development, and to develop independent perspectives" (Howell and Avolio 1992, p.49). Another paper by Sankowsky (1995) focuses on the abuse of power by narcissistic charismatics. Sankowsky (1995) contributed that narcissistic individuals "tend toward exploitative and manipulative behavior" (p.64) which "often leads to individual and collective poor performance" (pp.69-70) within organizations. In table 1 a summary of the relevant findings on follower's performance and job satisfaction is given.

Year	Author(s)	Findings		Relationship		Relevant findings
		Performance	Satisfaction	Positive	Negative	
1998	Shamir, Zakay, Breinin, Popper	X		X		Analysis of the impact of charismatic behavior in military units
1993	Yammarino, Spangler, Bass	X		X		Positive performance of midshipmen and their subsequent leaders at the USNA and of USN officers
1989	Howell and Frost	X		X		Participants of laboratory study that were lead by a charismatic individual achieved better task performances and higher task adjustments
2007	Cicero and Pierro	X	X	X		Positive relationship between charismatic leadership and employee's work-group identification
1996	Kirkpatrick and Locke	X		X		Positive performance of follower's quality and quantity in laboratory simulation with students in upper level business classes
1990	Seltzer and Bass		X	X		Positive influence on employees' job satisfaction under the condition of initiation and consideration
2006	Choi	X	X	X		Positive impact of charismatic leadership on followers' motivation, task performance and job satisfaction
1992	Howell and Avolio	X			X	Analysis of the effects of ethical and unethical charismatic leaders on their followers, unethical charismatic leaders undermine followers' motivation
1995	Sankowsky	X			X	Narcissistic charismatic leaders lead to individual and collective poor performance

Table 1: Summary of relevant findings on follower's performance and job satisfaction

3.1.2 Publications on organizational outcomes

More research effort has been conducted in terms of organizational outcomes. Numerous research scholars have found both theoretical and empirical evidence for positive relationships between charismatic leadership and organizational performance. Hater and Bass (1988) exposed positive theoretical results measuring the company performance at Federal Express (FedEx). Another contribution by Wilderom et al. (2012) specifically investigated the theoretical relationship of charismatic leadership and financial performance that also illustrated positive outcomes. In contrast Javidan and Waldman (2003) examined charismatic leadership in the Canadian public sector and concluded that such leadership is not related to organizational unit performance. In a study by Wilderom et al. (2012) an overview consisting of eleven publications that provided empirical evidence determining the relationship between charismatic leadership and several financial outcome indicators was given. This summary includes contributions that were published over the last 20 years. However, a twelfth paper examining similar issues was found in the literature. In only four of these studies significant empirical evidence was detected. These include Howell and Avolio (1993) by measuring business unit performance,

Geyer and Steyrer (1998) by analyzing long and short-term organizational outcomes, Rowold and Laukamp (2009) by evaluating organizations profit using the Conger Kanungo Scale as well as Agle and Sonnenfeld (1994) by researching chief executive officer (CEO) charisma on organizational performance in general. Five more studies delivered uncertain evidence for a relationship. Thereby, one Barling et al. (1996) discovered a positive relationship with personal loan sales, however only a slight relationship was found with credit card sales. Another study revealed empirical evidence for net profit and controllable costs in small-sized companies, but not in large enterprises (Koene et al. 2002). Waldman et al. (2004) presented a relationship for an increasing profit margin and return on investment, yet failed in delivering a positive relationship for growth in sales. In an earlier paper Waldman et al. (2001) studied the impact of charismatic CEO leadership on the financial performance in Fortune 500 enterprises. They proposed positive results on the financial "performance under conditions of uncertainty but not under conditions of certainty" (Waldman et al. 2001, p.134). Tosi et al. (2004) also used a sample of Fortune 500 firms and indicated that stock price returns are positively related to charismatic leadership, although this was not accurate for return on assets. Finally, three studies examining sales performance (Zhu et al. 2005), organizational profit (Rowold and Heinitz 2007) and future financial performance under consideration of uncertainty (Agle et al. 2006) failed to uncover any relationship with charismatic leadership.

In contrast, in his study "The dark side of leadership", Conger (1990) argued that the behavioral traits of charismatic leaders "produce problematic or even disastrous outcomes for their organizations" (p.44). Similarly, O'Connor et al. (1995) offered an empirical model of destructiveness on several characteristics to define personalized and socialized charismatic leadership. The analysis exhibited that personalized charismatic leaders exploit followers for personal gains and generate strong negative outcomes for the organization in the long run (O'Connor et al. 1995). The obtained findings in this study were similar to earlier papers focusing on destructive acts by personalized charismatics (e.g., Mumford et al. 1993). Table 2 provides a summary of the relevant findings discussing the relationship between charismatic leadership and organizational outcomes.

Year	Author(s)	Evidence		Significance of evidence			Relevant findings
		Theoretical	Empirical	Clear	Uncertain	Failed	
1988	Hater and Bass	X		X			Positve relationship to company performance at FedEx
2012	Wilderom, Van der Berg, Wiersma	X		X			Positive relationship to organizational financial performance
2003	Javidan and Waldman	X				X	No relationship to organizational unit performance in Canadian public sector
1993	Howell and Avolio		X	X			Positive relationship to business unit performance
1998	Geyer and Steyrer		X	X			Positive relationship to long and short-term organizational outcomes
2009	Rowold and Laukamp		X	X			Positive relationship to organizations profit
1994	Agle and Sonnenfeld		X	X			Positive relationship between CEO charisma and organizational performance in general
1996	Barling, Weber, Kelloway		X		X		Positive relationship with personal loan sales, slight relationship with credit card sales
2002	Koene, Vogelaar, Soeters		X		X		Positive relationship to net profit and controllable costs, only in small companies
2004	Waldman, Javidan, Varella		X		X		Positive relationship to increasing profit margin and ROI, not for growth in sales
2001	Waldman, Ramírez, House, Puranam		X		X		Postive relationship to financial performance under conditions of uncertainty in Fortune 500 firms, not under conditions of certainty
2004	Tosi, Misangyi, Fanelli, Waldman, Yammarino,		X		X		Positive relationship to stock price returns, not for ROA
2005	Zhu, Chew, Spangler		X			X	No relationship to sales performance
2007	Rowold and Heinitz		X			X	No relationship to organizational profit
2006	Agle, Nagarajan, Sonnenfeld, Srinivasan		X			X	No relationship to future financial performance under consideration of uncertainty
1990	Conger	X		X			Charismatic leadership leads to problematic or even disastrous organizational outcomes
1995	O'Connor, Mumford, Clifton, Gessner, Connelly	X		X			Charismatics exploit followers for personal gains and generate strong negative outcomes for the organization in the long run

Table 2: Summary of relevant findings on organizational outcomes

3.2 Comparison of different author's views

Based on the demonstrated exemplary studies and literature contributions the major scholars in the field of charismatic leadership can be identified. Howell (1988, 1989, 1992, 1993, 2005), House (1977, 1979, 1993, 2001) and Shamir (1993, 1998, 2005) seem to be the most important authors mainly discussing the positives effects on follower's performance and job satisfaction as well as on organizational outcomes. This is supported by theoretical and empirical evidence. In contrast, among a few others (e.g. Sankowsky 1995; O'Connor et al. 1995) Conger (1989, 1990, 1998) seems to be a lonely voice in disagreeing with the majority of authors. In his opinion charismatic leaders also possess a dark side that might lead to dramatically negative organizational outcomes and dissatisfaction in follower's job perception.

However, Conger published several studies in collaboration with Kanungo (1987, 1988, 1998) that contributed to the positive effects of charismatic leadership as well. That clearly shows that most major authors hold the opinion that there exists an overall positive relationship between charismatic leaders and outcomes even if a few scholars revealed different findings. Table 3 gives an overview of the scholars that agree or disagree on the examined topics.

Charismatic leadership is positively related to...	Authors that agree	Authors that disagree
follower's performance	Shamir et al. (1998); Yammarino et al. (1993); Howell and Frost (1989); Cicero and Pierro (2007); Kirkpatrick and Locke (1996); Choi (2006); Shamir et al. (1993); House (1977)	Howell and Avolio (1992); Sankowsky (1995)
follower's job satisfaction	Cicero and Pierro (2007); Seltzer and Bass (1990); Choi (2006)	
organizational outcome	Hater and Bass (1988); Wilderom et al. (2012); Howell and Avolio (1993); Geyer and Steyrer (1998); Rowold and Laukamp (2009); Agle and Sonnenfeld (1994); Barling et al. (1996); Koene et al. (2002); Waldman et al. (2004); Waldman et al. (2001); Tosi et al. (2004)	Javidan and Waldman (2003); Zhu et al. (2005); Rowold and Heinitz (2007); Agle et al. (2006); Conger (1990); O'Connor et al. (1995); Mumford et al. (1993)

Table 3: Comparison of different author's views

4 Identification of research gaps

Based on the previous review of literature three research gaps can be identified (Table 4).

| # | Research gap | Field of research | | Year | Author(s) |
		Follower	Organization		
1	Taking additional indicators into account that might be related to outcome criteria such as individual, team-level and organizational innovation		X	2009	Rowold and Laukamp
2	Including factors that interact as a mediating role between the behavior of leaders and followers such as followers' motivation		X	2009	Rowold and Laukamp
3	Investigation of motivational effects of personalized charismatic leaders	X		2006	Choi

Table 4: Overview of identified research gaps

Rowold and Laukamp (2009) identified two research gaps regarding studies that investigate the relationship between charismatic leadership and organizational performance. One research gap for future studies is to take additional indicators into account that might be related to outcome criteria. Particularly to mention is individual, team-level and organizational innovation.

Another research gap recognized by Rowold and Laukamp (2009) is to include factors that interact as a mediating role between the behavior of leaders and followers.

For instance follower's motivation could be considered as a further element to measure the impact on organizational performance. Both research gaps have not been properly covered by today.

Another area that future researchers should further continue to address is the dark side of personalized charismatic leaders (Samnani & Singh 2013). By abusing power personalized charismatics often negatively influence their follower's motivation as clarified by Sankowsky (1995). A particular research gap in this field is to investigate the motivational effects of personalized charismatic leaders (Choi 2006). So far scholars only examined the motivational effects of socialized charismatics. Even though Choi mentioned this gap in 2006, by today studies did not explore this subject matter sufficiently yet.

5 Conclusion

Even though most scholars published significant studies between 1980 and 2005 this article has demonstrated that overall a lot of research on the topic of charismatic leadership has been conducted. This shows that leadership is still a very important field of research in organizations.

To sum up it was highlighted that there has been many publications demonstrating that socialized charismatic leaders may have strong positive impacts on their followers. In turn there is theoretical and empirical evidence that charismatic individuals often lead to increasing organizational performance. Many scholars examined the relationship between charismatic leadership and numerous financial performance indicators within organizations and often concluded with either clear or tentative empirical results. However, even though "charismatic leadership clearly can enhance organizational performance, there is no guarantee of this effect" (Gardner & Avolio 1998, p.53).

Even if the majority of published work concentrates on the positive consequences a few scholars discussed the dark side of charisma and its negative influences on followers and the organization. These studies showed that personalized charismatic leaders tend to exploit their followers and may drastically harm organizational performance.

All in all "it seems obvious that charismatic leadership is neither inherently good nor evil, but the implicit assumption in the literature has been that it is a positive force in organizations" (Judge et al. 2006, p.204).

References

Agle, B.R., Nagarajan, N.J., Sonnenfeld, J.A. & Srinivasan, D. (2006): "Does CEO charisma matter? An empirical analysis of the relationships among organizational performance, environmental uncertainty, and top management team perceptions of CEO charisma", *Academy of Management Journal*, Vol. 49, 161–174.

Agle, B.R. & Sonnenfeld, J.A. (1994): "Charismatic chief executive officers: Are they more effective? An empirical test of charismatic leadership theory". *Academy of Management Best Papers Proceedings*, 2-6.

Antonakis, J. (2012): "Transformational and Charismatic Leadership" in *The Nature of Leadership*, ed. Day, D. V. and Antonakis, J., Thousand Oaks: SAGE Publications, Inc, 2nd Edition, 256-288.

Barling, J., Weber, T. & Kelloway, E.K. (1996): "Effects of transformational leadership training on attitudinal and financial outcomes: A field experiment", *Journal of Applied Psychology*, Vol. 6, 827–832.

Bass, B.M. (1985): *Leadership and performance beyond expectations*, New York: Free Press.

Bryman, A. (1992): *Charisma and Leadership in Organizations*, Newbury Park: Sage Publications.

Burke, W.W. (1986): "Leadership as empowering others" in *Executive power*, ed. Srivastva, S., San Francisco: Jossey-Bass, 51-77.

Choi, J. (2006): "A Motivational Theory of Charismatic Leadership: Envisioning, Empathy, and Empowerment", *Journal of Leadership and Organizational Studies*, Vol. 13, No. 1, 24-43.

Cicero, L. & Pierro, A. (2007): "Charismatic leadership and organizational outcomes: The mediating role of employees' work-group identification", *International Journal of Psychology*, Vol. 42, No. 5, 297–306.

Conger, J. (1989): *The charismatic leader: Behind the mystique of exceptional leadership*, San Francisco: Jossey-Bass.

Conger, J. (1990): "The dark side of leadership", *Organizational Dynamics*, Vol. 19, 44-55.

Conger, J.A. & Kanungo, R.N. (1987): "Toward a behavioral theory of charismatic leadership in organizational settings", *Academy of Management Review*, Vol. 12, No. 4, 637-647.

Conger, J. & Kanungo, R. (1998): *Charismatic Leadership in Organizations*, Thousand Oaks: SAGE Publications.

Gardner, W.L. & Avolio, B.J. (1998): "The charismatic relationship: A dramaturgical perspective", *Academy of Management Review*, Vol. 23, No. 1, 32-58.

Geyer, A.L.J. & Steyrer, J.M. (1998): "Transformational leadership and objective performance in banks", *Applied Psychology: An International Review*, Vol. 47, 397–420.

Hater, J.J. & Bass, B.M. (1988): "Supervisors' evaluations and subordinates' perceptions of transformational leadership", *Journal of Applied Psychology*, Vol. 73, 695-702.

Hayibor, S., Agle, B.R., Sears, G.J., Sonnenfeld, J.A. & Ward, A. (2011): "Value Congruence and Charismatic Leadership in CEO–Top Manager Relationships: An Empirical Investigation", *Journal of Business Ethics*, Springer, 237-254.

House, R.J. (1977): "A 1976 theory of charismatic leadership" in *Leadership*, ed. Hunt J. G., Larson L. L., Carbondale: University Press, 189–207.

House, R.J. & Baetz, M. (1979): "Leadership: Some empirical generalizations and new research directions" in *Research in organizational behavior*, ed. Staw, B. M., Vol. 1, Greenwich: JAI Press, 341-423.

Howell, J.M. (1988): "Two faces of charisma: Socialized and personalized leadership in organizations" in *Charismatic leadership: The elusive factor in organizational effectiveness*, ed. Conger J. A., Kanungo, R. N., San Francisco: Jossey-Bass, 213-236.

Howell, J.M. & Avolio, B. J. (1992): "The ethics of charismatic leadership: Submission or liberation?", *Academy of Management Executive*, Vol. 6, No. 2, 43-54.

Howell, J.M. & Avolio. B.J. (1993): "Transformational leadership, transactional leadership, locus of control, and support for innovation: Key predictors of consolidated-business-unit performance", *Journal of Applied Psychology*, Vol. 78, 891-902.

Howell, J.M. & Frost, P.J. (1989): "A Laboratory Study of Charismatic Leadership", *Organizational Behavior and Human Decision Processes*, Vol. 43, 243-269.

Howell, J.M. & Shamir, B. (2005): "The Role of Followers in the Charismatic Leadership Process: Relationships and their Consequences", *Academy of Management Review*, Vol. 30, No. 1, 96–112.

Javidan, M. & Waldman, D.A. (2003): "Exploring Charismatic Leadership in the Public Sector: Measurement and Consequences", *Public Administration Review*, Vol. 63, No. 2, 229-242.

Judge, T.A. & Fluegge Woolf, E., Hurst, C., Livingston, B. (2006): "Charismatic and Transformational Leadership: A Review and an Agenda for Future Research", *Zeitschrift für Arbeits- u. Organisationspsychologie*, Vol. 50, No. 4, 203-214.

Kirkpatrick, S.A. & Locke, E. A. (1996): "Direct and Indirect Effects of Three Core Charismatic Leadership Components on Performance and Attitudes", *Journal of Applied Psychology*, Vol. 81, No. 1, 36-51.

Koene, B.A.S., Vogelaar, A.L.W. & Soeters, J.L. (2002): "Leadership effects on organizational climate and financial performance: Local leadership effect in chain organizations", *The Leadership Quarterly*, Vol. 13, 193–215.

Mumford, M.D., Gessner, T.L., Connelly, M.S., O'Connor, J.A. & Clifton, T.C. (1993): "Leadership and destructive acts: Individual and situational influences", *Leadership Quarterly*, Vol. 4, 115-147.

O'Connor, J., Mumford, M.D., Clifton, T.C., Gessner, T.L. & Connelly, M.S. (1995): "Charismatic leaders and destructiveness: A historiometric study", *Leadership Quarterly*, Vol. 6, 529-555.

Rowold, J. & Heinitz, K. (2007): "Transformational and charismatic leadership: Assessing the convergent, divergent and criterion validity of the MLQ and the CKS", *Leadership Quarterly*, Vol. 18, 121-133.

Rowold, J. & Laukamp, L. (2009): "Charismatic leadership and objective performance indicators", *Applied Psychology: An International Review*, Vol. 58, 602–621.

Samnani, A. & Singh, P. (2013): "When leaders victimize: The role of charismatic leaders in facilitating group pressures", *The Leadership Quarterly*, Vol. 24, 189–202.

Sankowsky, D. (1995): "The charismatic leader as narcissist: Understanding the abuse of power", *Organizational Dynamics*, Vol. 23, 57-71.

Seltzer, J. & Bass, B.M. (1990): "Transformational Leadership: Beyond initiation and Consideration", *Journal of Management*, Vol. 16, No. 4, 693-703.

Shamir, B., House, R.J. & Arthur, M.B. (1993): "The motivational effects of charismatic leadership: A self-concept based theory", *Organizational Science*, Vol. 4, 577-594.

Shamir, B., Zakay, E., Breinin, E. & Popper, M. (1998): "Correlates of charismatic leader behavior in military units: Subordinates' attitudes, unit characteristics, and superiors' appraisals of leader performance", *Academy of Management Journal*, Vol. 41, 387-409.

Tosi, H.L., Misangyi, V. F., Fanelli, A., Waldman, D.A. & Yammarino, F.J. (2004): "CEO charisma, compensation and firm performance", *The Leadership Quarterly*, Vol. 15, 405–420.

Waldman, D.A., Javidan, M. & Varella,P. (2004): "Charismatic leadership at the strategic level: A new application of upper echelons theory", *The Leadership Quarterly*, Vol. 15, 355–380.

Waldman, D.A., Ramírez, G.G., House, R.J. & Puranam, P. (2001): "Does leadership matter? CEO leadership attributes and profitability under conditions of perceived uncertainty", *Academy of Management Journal*, Vol. 44, 134–143.

Weber, M. (1947): *The theory of social and economic organizations*, New York: Free Press.

Wilderom, C.P.M., Van der Berg, P.T & Wiersma, U.J. (2012): "A longitudinal study of the effects of charismatic leadership and organizational culture on objective and perceived corporate performance", *The Leadership Quarterly*, Vol. 23, 835-848.

Yammarino, F.J., Spangler. W.D. & Bass, B.M. (1993): "Transformational leadership and performance: A longitudinal investigation", *Leadership Quarterly*, Vol. 4, 81-102.

Yukl, G.A. (2010): *Leadership in Organizations*, Prentice Hall: Pearson, 7th edition, 262-277.

Yukl, G.A. (1999): "An evaluation of conceptual weakness in transformational and charismatic leadership theories", *The Leadership Quarterly*, Vol. 10, 285-305.

Zhu, W., Chew, I.K.H. & Spangler, W.D. (2005): "CEO transformational leadership and organizational outcomes: The mediating role of human-capital-enhancing human resource management", *The Leadership Quarterly*, Vol. 16, 39–52.

Humble Leadership

Katharina Sophie Vorwig, Felix Weichsel

Abstract. This article review on humble leadership is based on secondary data analysis and comprises a total of 61 sources, covering a wide range of empirical approaches, like theoretical expositions, practical case studies or quantitative and qualitative surveys. While scholars mainly disagree on a commonly used concept and definition of humility, there is some agreement concerning characteristics of humble leaders. Regarding measures for humility, the majority of authors focus on behavioral aspects and appearance of humble leaders, while others include both cognitive and motivational aspects. In addition, this article reveals that humble leader research is in a very early stage, in which clear theoretical foundations, a commonly agreed definition of the concept and widely accepted empirical evidence are missing. Notwithstanding scholars generally agree on the fact that it is a relevant topic, which gained increasing attention during recent years and receives growing interest in the future.

Keywords: Humble leaders, humble leadership, leader, humility and humbleness

1 Introduction

A famous Chinese philosopher once said "a leader is best when people barely know he exists, when his work is done, his aim fulfilled, they will say: we did it ourselves" (cf. Shinagel 2014). This emphasizes a leaders' character trait of being humble, which directly leads to the topic of this contribution.

For the purpose of presenting an overview of existing research about humble leaders it was decided to pursue an open search process for secondary data collection. In total, 61 sources were selected, covering a wide range of empirical approaches, such as theoretical expositions, practical case studies or quantitative and qualitative surveys.

This article presents existing literature about humble leaders by giving an overview on the research context and introducing selected research areas. A final section provides some concluding remarks and recommends future research areas based on existing research gaps.

2 Research Context and Integration

The concept of humility[1] has deep historical roots in the field of theology and philosophy (Templeton 1997; Grenberg 2005) and is yet discussed only little in management or business literature (e.g. Owens and Hekman 2012; Vera and Rodriguez-Lopez 2004). This may be based on the fact that humility was long mistakenly associated with low self-esteem during the 1980s (Weiss and Knight 1980, in Ou et al. 2014) and connected to missing confidence and ambition, as well as shy and passive behavior (Vera and Rodriguez-Lopez 2004). Nevertheless, it has turned into an increasingly important research topic particularly in the fields of both psychology and management (cf. Ou et al. 2014; Vera and Rodriguez-Lopez 2004).

Psychological research presents various measures of humility, particularly focusing on the positive in people and their characteristic traits (cf. Peterson and Seligman 2004; Rowatt et al. 2006; Exline and Geyer 2004; Davis et al. 2011).

By contrast, management research shows various streams and sub-categories. First and foremost, humility is discussed in several professional fields, such as law and jurisdiction (e.g. McConnell 1996; Scharffs 1998), medical professionalism (e.g. Butler et al. 2011; Lauer 2002), politics and military (e.g. Hughes 2010; Meyer 1997; Obama 2008) or religious settings (e.g. Chan et al. 2011; Kaufman 2012). Due to general constraints the scope of this article has been limited to research on humility in business settings. While some authors aimed at providing theoretical concepts for humility in leadership and organizations (cf. Morris et al. 2005; Vera and Rodriguez-Lopez 2004), others developed behavioral measures for humble leaders (Owens and Hekman 2012; Owens et al. 2013) or conducted studies in search and confirmation of conceptual or virtuous associations (Ashton and Lee 2005; Hackett and Wang 2012, Morris et al. 2005; Vera and Rodriguez-Lopez 2004).

---

[1] Despite the fact that some authors argue that "humility doesn't actually mean being humble" (Thompson and Tracy, 2010: 48), it can be resumed that the majority of researchers use these terminologies and their meanings interchangeably (cf. Exline and Geyer, 2004; Falk and Blaylock, 2012; Hayes and Comer, 2011; Morris et al., 2005; Nielsen et al., 2010; Ou et al., 2014; Owens and Hekman, 2012; Standish, 2007).

3 Research Areas of Humble Leaders

Today's research about humble leaders can be categorized in the following areas: Concept(s) and definitions (e.g. Collins 2001; Fry 2003; Van Dierendonck 2009), characteristics of humble leaders and humility (e.g. Morris et al. 2005; Owens and Hekman 2012; Tangney 2000, 2002), measures and perceptions (e.g. Exline and Geyer 2004; Rowatt et al. 2006), effects and effectiveness (e.g. Collins 2001a 2014; De Waal and Sivro 2012), as well as findings based on a lack of humility in leadership (e.g. Catterjee and Hambrick 2007; Malmendier and Tate 2005).

3.1 Concept(s) of Humility in Leadership

Various authors display their individual definitions and dimensions of humble leaders and humility in leadership. Hence, the concept is treated inconsistently and highly divergent.

Many researchers view humility as a personal and self-based trait, which is connected to leadership behavior and as such to humble leaders (Morris et al. 2005; Hackett and Wang 2012; Tangney 2002; Peterson and Seligman 2004). This enables a clear distinction between the leader as an individual with unique virtues and leadership as a behavioral component of the construct (DeRue et al. 2011).

On the contrary, there are researchers that follow a different approach, arguing that humility is *one* component of an existing leadership style (e.g. Caulkins 2008; Collins 2001b; Fry 2003; Van Dierendonck and Nuijten 2011; Patterson 2003) Though all of them include humility in their concept, they only take limited factors of the construct into account. Hence, it is not possible to distinguish between humility as a personal trait and humble leadership behavior; instead both elements are intertwined in their perspectives.

Collins (2001b 2014) presents the so-called Level 5 Leadership, stating that great companies require leaders that combine humility with fierce resolve and strength, since "good-to-great transformations don't happen without Level 5 leaders at the helm" (Collins 2001: 3), who combine a paradoxical mixture of professional will and personal humility.

Moreover, Greenleaf (1977) particularly coined the servant leadership style, which describes leaders that focus on the well-being and development of followers and thus encompasses an important aspect of humble leadership (cf. Graham 1991; Greenleaf and Spears 2002; Patterson 2003).

Van Dierendonck and colleagues (2009; Van Dierendonck and Nuijten 2001; Van Dierendonck et al. 2009) further illustrate that servant leaders are able to understand and assess their own achievements and talents, admitting that they can still learn and improve through knowledge of others, which again is associated with humble leader behavior.

Further concepts of leadership that are connected to humility in leadership, viewing the construct as *one* single component are the following: spiritual leadership (cf. Fry 2003), charismatic leadership (cf. Nielsen et al. 2010) or bottom-up approaches like follower-oriented leadership theories (cf. Matteson and Irving 2006; Weick 2001). Chang and Diddams (2009) take it one step further, arguing that humility equals authentic leadership, which is another leadership concept focusing on the alignment of one's internal self with external actions.

In addition, Caulkins (2008) possibly provides a basis for further research and re-theorizes Collins (2001a) culture of discipline. Thereby, Caulkins positions the culture of discipline in a broader context of existing cultures, eventually exploring humble and collaborative leadership as an alternative model to existing ones.

3.2 *Disagreed* Characteristics of Humility in Leadership

Regarding humble leader characteristics there is a distinction that can be drawn between agreed and disagreed traits, virtues and behaviors. Disagreement in particular arises from the group of authors that describe humility as *one* component of an overriding concept or pose other behaviors superior to being humble (e.g. Nielsen et al. 2010; Greenleaf and Spears 2002; Van Dierendonck 2011; Collins 2001a 2001b 2014). For instance, several authors argue that humility in leadership can be described as an "innate virtue, or personality traits" (Owens and Hekamn 2012: 789), which comprises self-awareness, self-transcendence (Morris et al. 2005), openness towards the new and personal knowledge or experience gaps, actively seeking feedback (Tangney 2002; Weick 2001; Peterson and Seligman 2004). Nielsen, Marrone and Slay (2010) further include the ability to self-assess ones weaknesses and strengths, as well as the tendency to look at others more than the self. In addition, servant leadership authors propose that humble leaders should be able to learn from their subordinates and be grateful for the "gifts of the less powerful" (Greenleaf and Spears 2002: 320). Other researchers define humility in distinction to narcissism, so self-focus and self-affirmation (Chatterjee and Hambrick 2007) or modesty and self-presentation (Peterson and Seligman 2004), disregarding certain characteristics like openness for new ideas or self-transcendence.

By characterizing humility as one important dimension of the Level 5 Leadership Collins (2001a 2001b 2014) emphasizes the mixture of personal humility and professional iron will, explaining that humble leaders show a lack of inspirational charisma, represent a kind of calmness and shyness, and believe that good luck is a success contributor. Collins "humble leaders" further incorporate a clear dedication towards the firm more than the self and the noble characteristic of never blaming collaborators or external effects for failure.

Additionally, there is also disagreement on the issue whether humility is an innate virtue (cf. Owens and Hekman 2012) a personal trait that can be developed over time (cf. Collins 2001a) or an aspirational process (Vera and Rodiguez-Lopez 2004). The last-named authors present an extensive list that describes humble leader behaviors, which involve aspirations for accepting others' failures, developing and respecting others, avoiding self-complacency or sharing rewards and achievements with collaborators. Yet further dimensions of humble leaders are frugality (Vera and Rodiguez-Lopez 2004), courtesy (Fry 2003), sincerity and fairness (Ashton and Lee 2005).

3.3 *Agreed* Characteristics of Humility in Leadership

By contrast, several researchers agree on characteristics that define humility in leadership and humble leaders as an autonomous concept itself. Besides, these authors emphasis various aspects but coincide with universal characteristics. Generally, humble leaders view themselves and others more objectively, appreciating strengths and accepting weaknesses, and are more open to new information and ideas (Exline and Geyer 2004; Owens et al. 2012; Tangney 2000 2002; Templeton 1997). Some even assume that there are probable benefits of humble leader behavior in practice (cf. Exline et al. 2004; Tangney 2000; Vera and Rodriguez-Lopez 2004), despite presenting appropriate measures and results in their work.

3.4 Measures and Perceptions of Humility in Leadership

Exline and Geyer (2004) complete a preliminary study about perceptions of the construct, questioning undergraduates regarding their associations and feelings about it. Interestingly, the authors conclude that despite the fact that humility was connected to positive emotions, personal strengths and success experiences, it was viewed as least favorable as a leader quality. This corresponds to Tangney (2000), who detects that people and dictionaries often describe humility in combination with low self-esteem, negative self-views, self-abasement and a feeling of worthlessness. The author resumes that even in the opposite case that people have positive feelings about humility, they can be reserved when it is ascribed to certain kinds of persons and situations; this again supports the earlier finding (cf. Exline and Geyer 2004).

In general, many researchers measure humility by focusing on behavioral aspects and appearance of humble leaders (Ashton and Lee 2005; Van Dierendonck 2011; Owens, Johnson and Mitchell 2013). By contrast, others include both cognitive and motivational aspects in their measurements (Tangney 2002; Peterson and Seligman 2004; Morris et al. 2005; Rowatt et al. 2006). In order to assess humble leaders, including Chief Executive Officers (CEOs) several researchers suggest that cognitive and motivational aspects are highly important in their decision-making processes and hence need to be considered (Finkelstein et al. 2009; Ou et al. 2014).

3.5 Establishing Humble Leadership

Based on qualitative research Owens and Hekman (2012) present the following process model that suggests one way of achieving humble leadership in organizations. The authors suggest to pursue two recommendations to reach the aimed outcome, that are legitimizing (1) the development journey of followers, including psychological freedom and engagement, and (2) the uncertainty to reinforce continuous small changes and ensure fluidity in the organization.

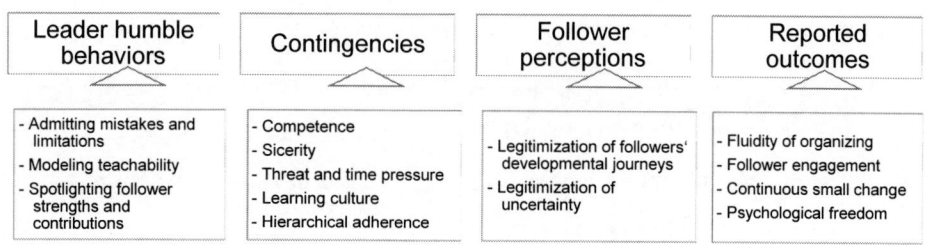

Figure 1: Process model adapted from Owens and Hekman (2012)

3.6 Effects of Humility in Leadership

Further research concerns the effectiveness of humble leader behavior in organizations and the relationship between humility and economic performance (cf. Caulkins 2008; Collins 2001a 2001b 2005; De Waal and Sivro 2012; Hayes and Comer 2011; Nuijten 2009; Ou et al. 2014; Van Dierendonck and Nuijten 2011; Dierendonck et al. 2009).

In this regard Collins (2001a 2001b) presents empirically proven material regarding the effectiveness of humble leaders based on level 5 leadership, turning him into a popular business guru in demand (Caulkins 2008). His results suggest a model for organizational development, in which organizations undergo various processes and actions, the so-called "good-to-great" transition, and eventually reach a stage of enduring and sustainable positive economic results. An important element of this model is disciplined people that are among others level 5 leaders (cf. Collins 2001b), who show humility in their leadership behavior. Thus, for an organization to become "great" and an industry's' benchmark with sustainable and long-lasting performance, humble leaders are a necessary condition. Moreover, Collins (2005) concept is not only applicable in business settings, but also in organizations within the non-profit and social sector, including religious and educational institutions, such as universities, churches or charities.

According to servant leadership literature humility may lead to improved organizational performance, however, there is no empirical evidence that supports this statement. Nevertheless, an indirect relationship through the use of mediating elements between the two components of servant leadership and organizational performance is ascertained (Nuijten 2009; Van Dierendonck and Nuijten 2011; Van Dierendonck et al. 2009). Other scholars however prove that employees are more content, engaged and better performing, when their leaders serve them (Liden, Wayne and Sparrowe 2000). De Waal and Sivro (2012) resume the above, finding an inconsistent role of servant leaders in relation to organizational performance.

Ultimately, there are other researchers that focus on specific effects of humility in leadership, such as outcome maximization for followers and their development (cf. Nielsen et al. 2010), opportunities for improved job performance and higher work engagement of CEO's and middle managers (Finkelstein et al. 2009; Ou 2012; Ou et al. 2014), as a necessity for firms to grow organically (cf. Hess 2007) or the possibility to use humility in building up a competitive advantage (cf. Vera and Rodriguez-Lopez 2004). The latter runs in direction of Collins research, though Vera and Rodriguez-Lopez focus more on organizational virtues rather than personal leader traits and only display examples that suggest humility as a key success factor for organizations and no empirical proof.

3.7 Effects of *Lacking* Humility in Leadership

Another research category for humble leaders represents the field of effects in case of lacking humility in leadership. Based on the fact that CEO characteristics affect organizations (Finkelstein et al. 2009), several researchers have explored the topic regarding self-aggrandizing CEOs, whose behavior can generally be viewed as contradicting to that of humble leaders. In this regard authors find that leaders that lack humility allow riskier investments (Malmendier and Tate 2005), agree on higher premium payments for acquisitions (Hayward and Hambrick 1997) and approve more dynamic and grand strategies that are more likely based on bad decision-making, resulting in fluctuating performance (Chatterjee and Hambrick 2007). Others emphasize that self-aggrandizing leaders are able to exercise unconstrained power (House and Aditya 1997), eventually leading to CEO failure (Dotlich and Cairo 2003). Research about real-life examples shows that lacking humility can reveal unbridled egos, hubris behavior, high self-importance (Boje et al. 2004; Knotterus et al. 2006) and personal failures (Falk and Blaylock 2012), which in return can have tremendous impact on the surroundings.

4 Concluding Remarks and Research Gaps

This review shows that literature about humble leaders can be separated in diverse research areas. While scholars mainly disagree on a commonly used concept and definition of humility, there is some agreement concerning its characteristics. Regarding measures for humility, the majority of authors focus on behavioral aspects and appearance of humble leaders, while others include both cognitive and motivational aspects. Further inconsistencies exist concerning effects and effectiveness of humble leaders, yet there is evidence that organizational and followers' performance is affected positively. By contrast, a lack of humility in leadership triggers undesirable outcomes, such as bad decision making and fluctuating performance.

This article reveals that humble leader research is in a very early stage, in which clear theoretical foundations, a commonly agreed definition of the concept and widely accepted empirical evidence are missing. Notwithstanding scholars generally agree on the fact that it is a relevant topic, which increasingly gained attention during recent years and further receives growing interest (e.g. Ou et al. 2014; Owens and Hekman 2012).

Since academics are in the very beginning of this topic, research gaps can be identified rather broadly, ranging from a clear definition of the concept and an understanding of how it influences people (both leaders and followers) to situational and external factors that cause a respective behavior or outcome or to clear insights on the influences it has on organizations, across hierarchical levels and the work process as such.

References

Ashton, M.C. and K. Lee (2005). Honesty-humility, the Big Five, and the Five-factor Model. Journal of Personality, Vol. 73: 1321-1353.

Boje, D. M., Roslie, G. A., Durant, R. A. and J. T. Luhman (2004). Enron spectacles: A critical dramaturgical analysis. Organization Studies, Vol. 25: 751-774.

Butler, P. D., Swift, M., Kothari, S., Nazeeri-Simmons, I., Friel, G. M., Longaker, M. T. and L. D. Britt (2011). Integrating cultural competency and humility train- ing into clinical clerk- ships: Surgery as a model. Journal of Surgical Education, Vol. 68: 222-230.

Chatterjee, A. and D. C. Hambrick (2007). It's all about me: Narcissistic CEOs and their effects on company strategy and performance. Administrative Science Quarterly, Vol. 52: 351-386.

Collins, J.C. (2001a). Good to Great: Why Some Companies Make the Leap…and Others Don't. New York: Harper Business.

Collins, J. (2001b). Level 5 Leadership – The Triumph of Humility and Fierce Resolve. Harvard Business Review. OnPoint 5831: 1-12.

Collins, J. (2005). Good to great and the social sectors. Boulder, CO: Jim Collins.

Collins, J. (2014). Jim Collins Homepage. Available under: http://www.jimcollins.com/ [Accessed: 03/14/14].

Caulkins, D. D. (2008). Re-theorizing Jim Collin's culture of discipline in *Good to Great*. Innovation: the European Journal of Social Science Research, Vol. 21 (3): 217-232.

Chan, C. A. C., McBey, K. and B. Scott-Ladd (2011) Ethical Leadership in Modern Employment Relationships: Lessons from St. Benedict. Journal of Business Ethics. Vol. 100: 221–228.

Chang, G. and M. Diddams (2009) Hubris or Humility: Cautious Surrounding the Construct and Self-definition of Authentic Leadershio. Academy of Management Annual Meeting Proceedings.

Davis, D. E., Hook, J. N., Worthington, E. L., Van Tongeren, D.R., Gartner, A. L., Jennings, D. J. and R. A. Emmons (2011). Relational humility: Conceptualizing and measuring humility as a personality judgement. Journal of Personality Assessment, Vol. 93: 225-234.

De Waal, A. and M. Sivro (2012). The Relation Between Servant Leadership, Organizational Performance, and the High-Performance Organization Framework. Journal of Leadership & Organizational Studies Vol. 19 (2): 173-190.

DeRue, D. S., Nahrgang, J. D., Wellman, N. and S. E. Humphrey (2011). Trait and behavioural theories of leadership: An integration and meta-analytic test of their relative validity. Personnel Psychology, Vol. 64: 7-52.

Dotlich, D. and P. Cairo (2003). Why CEO's fail. San Francisco: Jossey-Bass.

Exline, J. J., Campbell, W. K., Baumeister, R. F., Joiner, T., Krueger, J., and L.V. Kachorek (2004). Humility and modesty (461-475) In Peterson, C. and M. Seligman (Eds.), The values in action (VIA) classification of strengths. Cincinnati, OH: Values in Action Institute.

Exline, J. J. and A. L. Geyer (2004). Perceptions of Humility: A Preliminary Study. Self and Identity, Vol. 3: 95-114.

Falk, C. F. and B. K. Blaylock (2012). The H Factor: A Behavioral Explanation of Leadership Failures in the 2007-2009 Financial System Meltdown. Journal of Leadership, Accountability and Ethics, Vol. 9 (2): 68-77.

Finkelstein, S., Hambrick, D. C. and A. A. Cannella (2009). Strategic Leadership: Theory and Research on Executives, Top Manaement Teams, and Boards. Oxford: Oxford University Press.

Fry, L. W. (2003). Toward a theory of spiritual leadership. Leadership Quarterly, Vol. 14: 693-727.

Graham, J. W. (1991). Servant leadership in organizations: Inspirational and moral. Leadership Quarterly, Vol. 2 (2): 105-119.

Greenleaf, R. K. (1977). Servant leadership: A journey into the nature of legitimate power and greatness. New York, NY: Paulist Press.

Greenleaf, R. K. and L.G. Spears (2002). Servant leadership: A journey into the nature of legitimate power and greatness. Mahwah, NJ: Paulist Press.

Grenberg, J. (2005). Kant and the Ethics of Humility: A Story of Dependence, Corruption, and Virtue. Cambridge (UK): Cambridge University Press.

Hackett, R. D. and G. Wang (2012). Virtues and leadership: An integrating conceptual framework founded in Aristotelian and Confucian perspectives on virtues. Management Decision, Vol. 50: 868-899.

Hayes, M. and M. Comer (2011) Lead With Humility. Build trust and inspire others!. Leadership Excellence, Vol. 28 (9): 13.

Hayward, X. and D. C. Hambrick (1997). Explaining premiums paid for large acquisitions: Evidence of CEOs hubris. Administrative Science Quarterly, Vol. 42: 103-127.

Hess, E. D. (2007). Humble Leaders. They get great organic growth. Leadership Excellence, Vol. 24 (5): 10.

House, R. J. and R. N. Aditya, X. (1997) The social scientific study of leadership: Quo vadis?. Journal of Management, Vol. 23: 409-473.

Hughes, L. W. (2010). Leadership under pressure: Tactics from the front line. Leadership and Organization Development Journal, Vol. 31: 187-188.

Kaufman, P. I. (2012) Humility, civility, and vitality: Papal leadership at the turn of the seventh century. Leadership, Vol. 8 (3): 245-256.

Knotterus, J. D., Ulsperger, J. S., Cummins, S. and E. Osteen (2006). Exposing Enron, Media representations of ritualized deviance in corporate culture. Crime, Media, Culture: An International Journal, Vol. 2 (2): 177-195.

Lauer, G. S. (2002). Tbe basic recipe for a leader. Modern Healthcare, 32-33.

Liden, R. C., Wayne, S. J. and R. T. Sparrowe, R. T. (2000). An examination of the mediating role of psychological empowerment and the relation between job, interpersonal relationships, and work outcomes. *Journal of Applied Psychology*, Vol. *85*: 407-416.

Malmendier, U. and G. Tate (2005). CEO overconfidence and corporate investment. Journal of Finance, Vol. 60: 2661-2700.

Matteson, J. A. and J. A. Irving (2006). Servant versus self-sacrificial leadership: A behavioural comparison of two follower-oriented leadership theories. International Journal of Leadership Studies, Vol. 2: 36-51.

McConnell, M. W. 1996. Tbe importance of bumility in judicial review: A comment on Ronald Dworkin's "moral reading" of the constitution. Fordham Law Review, 65:1269-1293.

Meyer, E. G. (1997). Leadership: A return to basics. Military Review, Vol. 77: 58-61.

Morris, J. A., Brotheridge, C. M. and J. C. Urbanski (2005). Bringing humility to leadership: Antecedents and consequences of leader humility. Human Relations, Vol. 58 (10): 1323-1350.

Nielsen, R., Marrone, J. A. and H. S. Slay (2010). A New Look at Humility: Exploring the Humility Concept and Its Role in Socialized Charismatic Leadership. Journal of Leadership & Organizational Studies, Vol. 17 (1): 33-43.

Nuijten, I. (2009). Servant leadership: Paradox or diamond in the rough? A multidimensional measure and empirical evidence (Doctoral dissertation). Vrije Universiteit Amsterdam, Amsterdam, Netherlands.

Obama, B. (2008). Renewing American leadership. Foreign Affairs, Vol. 86: 2-16.

Ou, A. Y. (2012). Building Empowering Organization: A Study of Humble CEOs. Academy of Management Annual Meeting Proceedings.

Ou, A. Y., Tsui, A. S., Kinicki, A. J., Waldman, D. A., Xiao, Z. and L. J. Song (2014). Humble Chief Executive Officers' Connections to Top Management Team Integration and Middle Managers' Responses. Administrative Science Quarterly, Vol. 59 (1): 34-72.

Owens, B. P. and D. R. Hekman (2012). Modeling How to Grow: An Inductive Examination of Humble Leader Behaviors, Contingencies, and Outcomes. Academy of Management Journal, Vol. 55 (4): 787-818.

Owens, B.P., Johnson M. D., and T. R. Mitchell (2013). Expressed humility in organizations: Implications for performance, teams, and leadership. Organization Science, Vol. 24: 1517-1538.

Patterson, K. (2003). Servant Leadership: A Theoretical Model. Servant Leadership Roundtable, School of Leadership Studies, Regent University. Virgina Beach (VA).

Peterson, C. and M. E. P. Seligman (2004). Character Strengths and Virtues: A Handbook and Classification. Washington, DC: American Psychological Association, New York: Oxford University Press.

Rowatt, W. C., Powers, C., Targhetta, V., Comer, J., Kennedy, S. and J. Labouff (2006). Development and initial validation of an implicit measure of humility relative to arrogance. The Journal of Positive Psychology, Vol. 1 (4): 198–211.

Scharffs, B. (1998). The role of humility in exercising practical wisdom. University of California, Davis, Law Review, Vol. 32: 127-199.

Shinagel, M. (2014). The Paradox of Leadership. Harvard blog: The Language of Business. Available under: http://www.dce.harvard.edu/professional/blog/paradox-leadership [Accessed: 03/01/14].

Standish, N.G. (2007). Humble Leadership: Being Radically Open to God's Guidance and Grace. Alban Institute.

Tangney, J. P. (2000). Humility: Theoretical perspectives, empirical findings, and directions for future research. Journal of Social and Clinical Psychology, Vol. 19 (1): 70–82.

Tangney, J. P. (2002). Humility (411-419). In Snyder, C.R. (Ed.) Handbook of Positive Psychology. New York: Oxford University Press.

Templeton, J. M. (1997). Worldwide Laws of Life. Philadelphia: Templeton Foundation Press.

Thompson, M. and B. Tracy (2010). Building a great organization. Article adapted from: Now, Build a Great Business!. Leader to Leader Institute. 45-49.

Van Dierendonck, D. (2011). Servant Leadership: A Review and Synthesis. Journal of Management Vol. 37 (4): 1228-1261.

Van Dierendonck, D. and I. Nuijten, (2011). The servant leader- ship survey: Development and validation of a multidimensional measure. Journal of Business and Psychology, Vol. 26, 249-267.

Van Dierendonck, D., Nuijten, I., and I. Heeren (2009). Servant leadership, key to follower well-being (319-337).. In D. Tjosvold & B. Wisse (Eds.), Power and interdependence in organizations. New York. NY: Cambridge University Press.

Vera, D. and A. Rodriguez-Lopez (2004). Strategic virtues: Humility as a source of competitive advantage. Organizational Dynamics, Vol. 33 (4): 393–408.

Weick, K.E. (2001). Leadership as legitimization of doubt (91-102) In: Bennis, W., Spreitzer, G. M. and T. G. Cummings (Eds.) The Future of Leadership: Today's Top Leadership Thinkers Speak to Tomorrow's Leaders. San Francisco: Jossey-Bass.

Section II: Coaching

Leadership Coaching

Simon Knoll, Cormac Stafford, Debora Benson

Abstract. Although leadership coaching achieved considerable significance over the preceding years, it's popularity did not lead to the same effort in research. Currently, research articles mainly constitute practitioner articles focusing on best practice, without the verification of any research findings. Nevertheless, some quantitative research on leadership coaching exists, facilitating a fundamental understanding of the topic. Leadership coaching thereby defines a relationship between client and coach to improve the client's leadership abilities through a supported process. An important factor in leadership coaching is the alignment of individual and organizational goals through experiencing transformational change. The coach, the coachee and the relationship of the two therefore need to fit and follow a mutual agenda. As long as trust, commitment and objective feedback from coaches and corporations are provided, leadership coaching accelerates individual performance and creates a competitive advantage for organizations. Although literature regarding leadership coaching is increasing, this examination revealed four vital research gaps. Future research should hence aim to close these gaps to strengthen the practical understanding of leadership coaching and to enhance the outcomes of leadership coaching agreements.

Keywords: Leadership, coaching, self-awareness, 360 degree feedback, on-board coaching, executive coaching, leadership coaching, leadership development

1 Introduction

Of late, leadership coaching has achieved significant relevance (Popper & Lipshitz 1992; Larson & Richburg 2003) apparent in the myriads of leadership coaches being hired over the last years (Day, Surtees, & Winkler 2008; Bolch 2001). Unfortunately, this popularity did not lead to the same effort in leadership coaching research (Latham 2007).

Identifying essential research findings in leadership coaching presents a challenge since most articles contain unverified practitioner thoughts on best practice (e.g. Goldsmith "Expanding the Value of Coaching" 2012; Koltin 2013; Riddle & Ting 2006; Hawkins 2009; Harper 2012). Few authors conducted quantitative measures to validate their findings (MacKie 2007). This limited empirical research stream concentrates either on (1) evaluating leadership coaching in an holistic routine (e.g.

De Meuse & Dai 2009; Berg & Karlsen 2012), (2) comparing the performance of coaching participants and non-coaching participants (e.g. Hernez-Broome 2002), or (3) determining the results of coaching on a personal level (e.g. Bower 2012). Consequently, leadership coaching signifies a rather new, unexplored method to develop future leaders (Boyce, Jackson, & Neal 2010).

The objective of this article is the identification of best practice while still emphasizing the research gaps and insufficient fields of research governing leadership coaching. The structure of the paper is threefold and visualized in Figure 1: The first chapter defines leadership coaching and delimits it against (1) Consulting, (2) Counseling, (3) Mentoring and (4) Therapy. The second section contains the literature review, which reveals basic factors of leadership coaching and shows differing thoughts from literature. Finally, a critical assessment of the published literature is provided, together with concluding statements on leadership coaching.

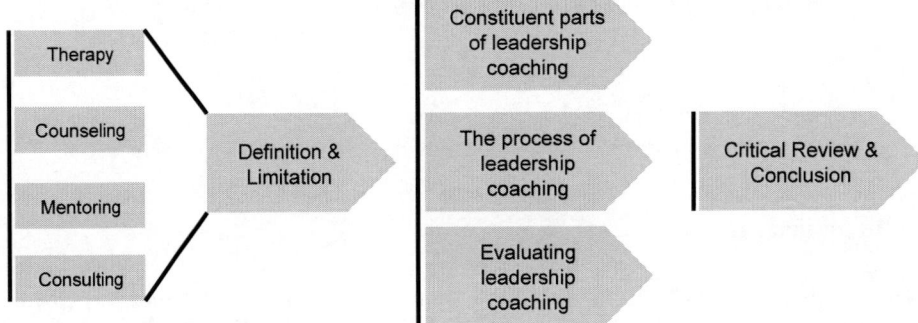

Figure 1: Structure of the article

1.1 Definition of Leadership Coaching

In literature, different definitions of coaching are found (see Exhibit 2). This paper defines leadership coaching as the relationship of client and coach to improve the efficiency of the client's pre-acquired abilities (e.g. Popper & Lipshitz 1992) through facing challenging situations in a supported process (Berg & Karlsen 2012) to develop the ability to "articulate visions, embodying values, and creating the environment within which things can be accomplished" (Richards & Engle 1986, p. 206). In this setting, "the person being coached (coachee) defines the agenda and the coach serves as a committed listener, active inquirer and instrument of change" to emphasize improvements of performance (Watt 2004, p. 15). Incorporating Bandura's (1977) social learning theory defines leadership coaching as an enhancement of a trainee's psychological development (Popper & Lipshitz 1992) through a dynamic process of creativity and innovation (Kets de Vries 2008) to obtain strategic objectives (Larson & Richburg 2003).

1.2 Delimitation of Leadership Coaching

The terminologies leadership coaching, consulting (Coutu & Kauffman 2009), therapy (Bluckert 2005), mentoring (Watt 2004; Barnett 1995) and counseling (Bluckert 2005; Popper & Lipshitz 1992) are often used interchangeably in literature. However, leadership coaching embodies a separate and unique technique of leadership development (Fielden 2005). Interestingly, different models exist classifying coaching between two or more areas of personal interaction (Coutu & Kauffman 2009; West & Milan 2001; see Exhibit 3 & Exhibit 4). Greene and Grant's (2003) framework (see Figure 1) integrates these models and delimits coaching from mentoring, therapy, consulting and counseling by the distinguishing factors of the number of clients (Hawkins 2009) – coachee, organization and the relationship between the two – and the process of developing leadership skills (Watt 2004).

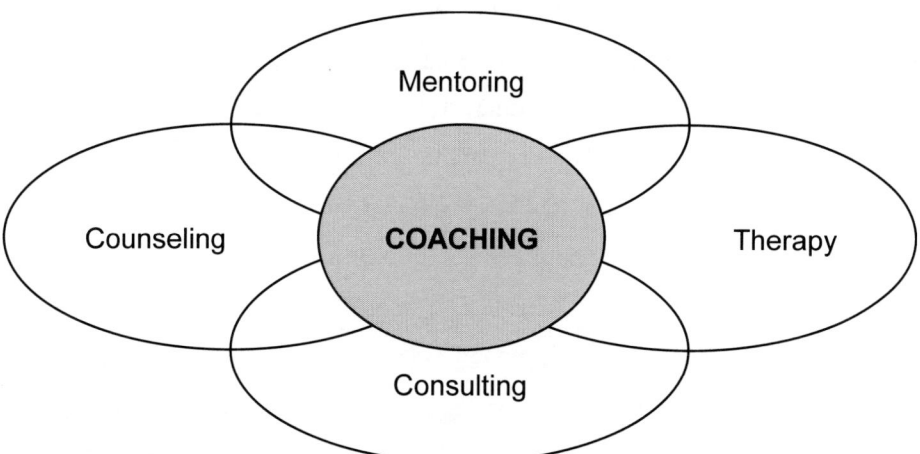

Figure 2: Greene and Grant model

2 Literature Review

Leadership coaching underwent vast development in the past and illustrates a clinical approach to leadership development based on previously assimilated skills and abilities (Day, Surtees, & Winkler 2008). Yet, authors could not verify many findings on leadership coaching nor were they able to identify any ideal setting for leadership coaching (Coutu & Kauffman 2009). This chapter is hence committed to numerous academic findings and evaluates their conformity or disconformity in the general context of leadership coaching defined in Chapter 1.

2.1 Constituent parts of leadership coaching

2.1.1 The Coach

The leadership coach is inevitably an important contributor to the coaching engagement (Harper 2012) since he ensures an environment of trust and support in which a coachee can excel (Popper & Lipshitz 1992). Researchers suggest different set of skills for a coach to maximize the benefit of leadership coaching (e.g. Koltin 2013; Harper 2012; Orth, Wilkinson, & Benfa 1987). Clearly, the personal skill-set as well as practical coaching experience are understood to be essential. Jarvis (2004) categorized the evaluation criteria for coaches described in the available literature. Her results can be compressed to the level of experience, coaching skills and relational factors such as supervision and boundary setting. Nevertheless, so far researchers could not confirm the optimal skill set of coaches nor were they able to embrace experience and age in their research papers.

RESEARCH GAP 1: Lack of research concerning the optimal skill-set/experience of a leadership coach

Aside from the optimal skill-set of coaches, researchers disagree on the embedding of leadership coaches within an organization (Watt 2004). Hall, Otazo, & Hollenbeck (1999) segregate internal and external coaches according to their coaching background, within or from outside the company, and emphasize the former to be used for quick interventions whereas the latter are appropriate for confidential coaching agreements. Other scholars provide additional reasons for using internal or external coaches (see Table 1) but so far no empirical study has addressed this comparison.

External coaches are preferable in providing:	Internal coaches are preferable in providing:
Sensitive feedback in an organization (Kets de Vries 2008)	Knowledge of the company and its history (Boyce, Jackson & Neal 2010)
Specialized expertise (Jarvis 2004)	Support through availability (Watt 2004)
Confidentiality (Boyce, Jackson & Neal 2010)	Task-oriented support (Watt 2004)
Experience in leadership coaching (Watt 2004)	High levels of trust (Boyce, Jackson & Neal 2010)
Objective feedback (Larson & Richburg 2007)	Cheap but sufficient leadership coaching (Kets de Vries 2008)

Table 1: Listing of scholars categorizing internal and external coaches

RESEARCH GAP 2: Lack of research evaluating internal/external leadership coaching

2.1.2 The Coaching Respondent

Originally, in leadership coaching, the coaching respondent (coachee) was involved in a one-on-one process to improve certain abilities (Hall, Otazo, & Hollenbeck 1999) but lately peer coaching (Parker, Hall, & Kram 2008), leadership team coaching (Day & Harrison 2007) and even organizational leadership coaching have been applied (Kets de Vries 2008) expanding the original spectrum of leadership coaching.

Although leadership coaching can theoretically be conducted with any person, evaluating a participant's coachability (see Exhibit 5) is essential in determining and ensuring personal motivation to avoid any waste of resources (Larson & Richburg 2003).

Starting on the individual level, people with average self-confidence respond best to leadership coaching since they are critical of their behavior but confident of their strengths (Hogan & Warrenfeltz 2003). Notably, young people react particularly positively to leadership coaching, whereas more challenges appear at later ages (Popper & Lipshitz 1992). Hence, schools, colleges and universities offer a primary opportunity to prepare future leaders (Calkins 1945). Business Schools and MBA-programs, especially, can provide significant structures to develop true leaders (Petriglieri, Wood, & Petriglieri 2011).

The INSEAD Global Leadership Center (IGLC), one of the biggest and most renowned Business Schools in the world, favors group coaching (Kets de Vries 2008) since "personal transformation is enhanced by vicarious learning from the examples of others" (p. 15). The identification of similar goals and the acknowledgement of equivalent circumstances and challenges support team and individual performance (Day & Harrison 2007; Hernez-Broome 2002). Contrary to the expectations, Sue-Chan and Latham's (2004) research, however, revealed an inferior effectiveness of peer coaching compared to self- and professional one-to-one coaching.

On an organizational level, leadership coaching is seen as a corporate culture emphasizing individual and organizational growth through continuous learning to develop employees (Larson & Richburg 2003). Performance improvement thereby starts with the C-Suite establishing continuous leadership coaching to permeate every branch with the associated benefits (Kets de Vries 2008). Although many scholars foster team and organizational leadership coaching, no empirical evidence supporting the benefit of group and organizational coaching over individual coaching has been found.

RESEARCH GAP 3: Lack of research comparing the benefits of group and organizational leadership coaching with individual leadership coaching

2.1.3 The Coaching Relationship

The relationship between a coach and a coachee exhibits the third component of leadership coaching. The coaching progression is most effective when coachees participate in the matching process (Boyce, Jackson, & Neal 2010) and when relationships between coaches and coachees are established at an emotional level (Parker, Hall, & Kram 2008).

In order to maximize leadership coaching effectiveness, the fit of coach and coachee needs to be guaranteed (Goldsmith, Lyons, Freas, & Witherspoon 2000). Since organizations aim to improve a coachee's performance, they need to find the right match for both the organization and the individual (Larson & Richburg 2003). Even if leadership coaching were only concerned with a single person, a rigorous and careful process is required to maximize its value (Jarvis 2004).

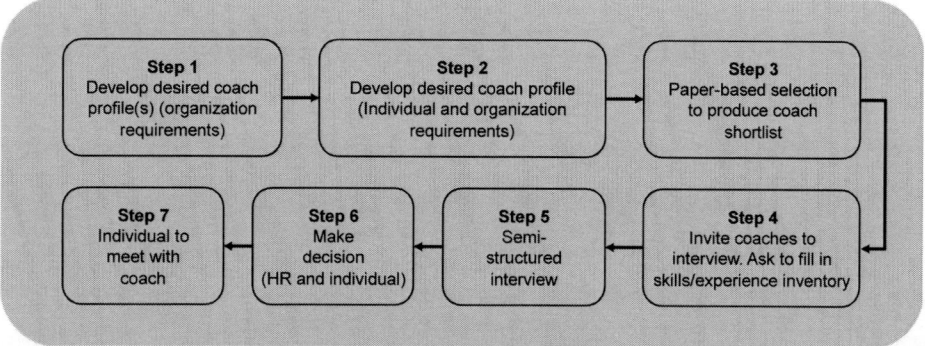

Figure 3: Coach selection process when recruiting a single coach (Jarvis 2004)

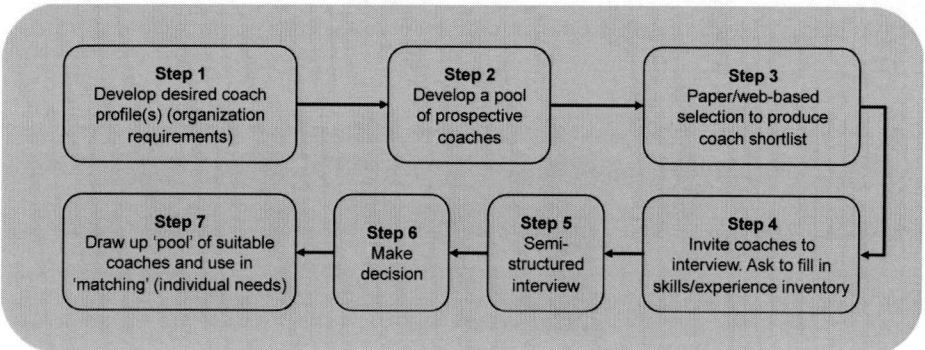

Figure 4: Coach selection process when recruiting a team coach (Jarvis 2004)

After selecting and contracting a coach, the coaching relationship between coach and coachee has to be established by defining the conditions of their collaboration (Chiumento 2007) and by delimiting their relationship to a professional dimension (Horner 2002). Based on the contract, coaches and coachees are then able to undertake their engagement and start working towards their objectives. Larson and Richburg (2007) thereby emphasize the "7 C's of Successful Coaching" (Context, Clarity, Commitment, Coachability, Courses of Action, Confidentiality, and Chemistry), which should build on mutual conformity to accelerate transformational or behavioral change. In addition to the "7 C's of Successful Coaching", culture portrays another important factor (Donnison 2008). Matching requirements and common ideals, as well as having similar objectives as a foundation of coaching relationships, increase the efficacy of leadership coaching in general.

2.2 The Process of Leadership Coaching

There is a wealth of literature focusing on ideal processes for leadership coaching (e.g. Hawkins 2009; Pearce 2007). Correspondingly, dozens of models and frameworks (e.g. Inner Game Model, Grow Model, Team Coaching Model) were developed but none captures a holistic, uniform applicability incorporating coachees' individuality and preceding development.

Goldsmith's (2000) 4-step model of leadership coaching, for example, facilitates assessing the abilities of coachees in the beginning, to subsequently determine the effectiveness of the engagement. Thereafter, establishing an action plan and publicly announcing objectives of the engagement increases the commitment of participants and enforces motivation to change (Latham 2007). The last stage concerns the incremental implementation of the acknowledgements, in daily life, through the process of performance optimization (Parker, Hall, & Kram 2008), emotional intelligence (Kets de Vries 2008) and transformational change (Hoover, Giambatista, Sorenson, & Bommer 2010). Mastering all four steps enforces lifelong behavioral change (Goldsmith, Lyons, Freas, & Witherspoon 2000) through critical self-reflection (Petriglieri, Wood, & Petriglieri 2011) supported by coaches mirroring performances from different perspectives (Kets de Vries 2008). The coachee thereby improves and channels existing leadership skills, which will then become present in any circumstance in life.

2.3 The Effectiveness of Leadership Coaching

Evaluating the effectiveness of leadership coaching creates a challenge since outcomes, that are not directly measureable, need to be observed. In general, training interventions are rarely evaluated in terms of achieving professed goals (Hogan & Warrenfeltz 2003) and to date, no universally accepted evaluation criteria for leadership coaching has been developed (MacKie 2007). However, it is commonly agreed that leadership coaching aligns individual and organizational objectives to increase efficiency (Hawkins 2009) while embracing more valuable decisions (Jarvis 2004).

Assessments of leadership coaching need to contrast initial and subsequent competencies to measure direct improvements (Hogan & Warrenfeltz 2003). Attempts are growing in which Returns on Investments (ROI) or costs for not undertaking leadership coaching (e.g. Anderson 2001; Larson & Richburg 2003; see Exhibit 6) are analyzed. Yet, critics focus on the questionable assertion that these figures are attributable to the long-term effect of leadership coaching, and on the inability to assess results in monetary terms (Berg & Karlsen 2012). Instead of calculating monetary values, leadership coaching can more easily be evaluated and sustained through feedback (MacKie 2007) assessing (1) intrapersonal, (2) interpersonal, (3) leadership, and (4) business skills (Hogan & Warrenfeltz 2003). However, the downsides of evaluating coaching efforts on qualitative responses are the over- and underestimation of abilities owing to subjective observations (De Meuse & Dai 2009). Recourse to 360-degree feedback, incorporating different stakeholders of the coachee in the evaluation process, balances over- and underestimations, resulting in more realistic evaluations (Thach 2002). Kirkpatrick's (1996) Four-Level Model provides an ideal setting to evaluate leadership coaching through 360-degree feedback. The model comprises four evaluation criteria ranging from reactions towards the coaching engagement, over-measuring the learning outcome and behavioral change, to analyzing results in terms of increased sales or higher productivity. Adjusting this model to leadership coaching could provide a holistic dimension to leadership coaching evaluation.

RESEARCH GAP 4: Lack of research evaluating leadership coaching in a universal model

3   Critical Review and Conclusion

Although myriads of articles exist on leadership coaching and although leadership coaching is conducted in more than 80 percent of organizations, across all sectors (Day, Surtees, & Winkler 2008), the profession is still at the early stages of development (Bluckert 2005). So far, only little quantitative research has been conducted to analyze the best practices recommended by practitioners. However, since leadership coaching is receiving vast attention lately, more empirical research on this topic will follow, defining the ideal setting for leadership coaching and closing the research gaps, which are currently observable.

3.1 The Ideal State of Leadership Coaching

Deriving from present literature, ideal leadership coaching is founded on a supportive relationship promoting challenging situations to engage coachees in a process of self-reflection, initiating transformational change. High engagement of both coach and coachee maximize intrinsic motivation and facilitate a constant learning process, creating acceptance of leadership coaching at an organizational level. Continuous 360-degree feedback and additional objective feedback from coaches, as well as large support from organizations and managers, align the objectives of individuals and organizations, which in turn lead to increased performance of both individuals and organizations (see Exhibit 7). Sustaining leadership coaching over an extended period of time subsequently creates a corporate coaching culture, facilitating an organization-wide performance improvement, which can reinforce competitive advantages.

Research Gaps in Leadership Coaching	References to Research Gap	Research Ideas
Lack of research concerning the optimal skill-set/experience of a leadership coach	De Meuse 2009	Undertake a research study measuring coaches from different backgrounds and their impact on coachees
Lack of research evaluating internal/external leadership coaching	Jarvis 2004	Undertake a research study comparing internal and external coaches' impact on coachees
Lack of research comparing the benefits of group and organizational leadership coaching with individual leadership coaching	Larson & Richburg 2003	Compare the impact of group coaching and organizational coaching with individual coaching
Lack of research evaluating leadership coaching in a universal model	Latham 2007	Adjusting Krikpatrick's Four-Level-Model to leadership coaching and measure the result through 360-degree feedback

Table 2: References of research gaps in current studies on leadership coaching

3.2 Current Gaps in Research

While examining the literature on leadership coaching, four areas of contradictory or missing research were identified (see Table 2). Firstly, empirical studies relating the skill-set and experience of a leadership coach to its efficacy were not found. Secondly, quantitative measures comparing internal and external coaches were not available in literature. Thirdly, sufficient research on the benefits of leadership group coaching and organizational leadership coaching, compared to individual coaching, have yet to be published. Similarly, current research lacks an adequate model or framework to measure the efficacy of leadership coaching in a universal manner incorporating different developmental stages of coachees. Future researches may therefore aim to fill the identified gaps and clarify the field of leadership coaching.

3.3 Change as a Drawback to Leadership Coaching

Change represents the major resistance of organizations and individuals towards leadership coaching (Kegan & Lahey 2009). Reasons for the resistance can be widespread as the Conceptual Model of Kets de Vries (2008) shows (see Figure 5). But change is not the only challenge for leadership coaching. The applicability of theory and practice (Barker 1997), the belief that coaching is nonsense (Jarvis 2004) or the subsequent return to former patterns of behavior (Barker 1997) provide just a selection of factors exemplifying the difficulties of delivering leadership coaching. Since these biases may not be detected at first sight, leadership coaching can face very challenging situations, although theoretically providing value to its participants.

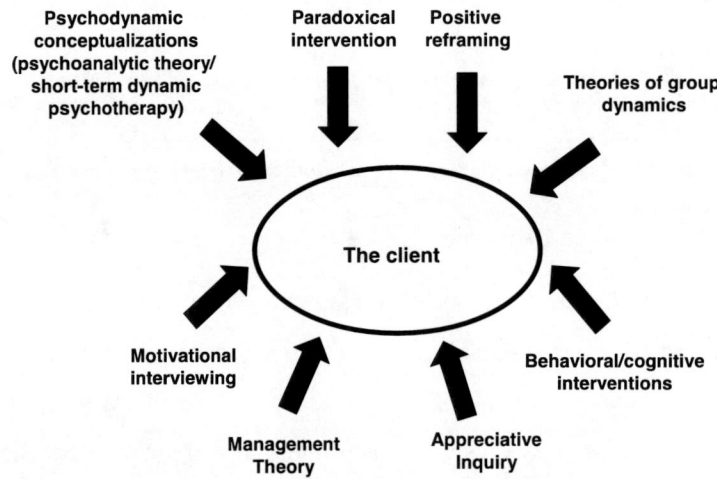

Figure 5: Influences of change on a coaching client (Kets de Vries 2008)

Appendix

Exhibit 1

Articles	Empirical	Non-empirical
(Anderson, 2001)	X	
(Bandura, Social Learning Theory, 1977)		X
(Barker, 1997)		X
(Barnett, 1995)		X
(Berg & Karlsen, 2012)	X	
(Bluckert, 2005)		X
(Bolch, 2001)		X
(Bower, 2012)	X	
(Boyce, Jackson, & Neal, 2010)	X	
(Calkins, 1945)		X
(Chiumento, 2007)		X
(Coutu & Kauffman, 2009)	X	
(Day & Harrison, 2007)		X
(De Meuse & Dai, 2009)	X	
(Donnison, 2008)		X
(Fielden, 2005)		X
(Goldsmith, Expanding the Value of Coaching, 2012)		X
(Goldsmith, Future Leaders How can we help them?, 2010)		X
(Goldsmith, Lyons, Freas, & Witherspoon, 2000)		X
(Greene & Grant, 2003)		X
(Hackman & Wageman, 2007)		X
(Hall, Otazo, & Hollenbeck, 1999)		X
(Harper, 2012)		X
(Hawkins, 2009)		X
(Hernez-Broome, 2002)		X
(Hogan & Warrenfeltz, 2003)		X
(Hoover, Giambatista, Sorenson, & Bommer, 2010)	X	
(Horner, 2002)		X
(Jarvis, 2004)	X	
(Kegan & Lahey, 2009)		X
(Kets de Vries, 2008)		X
(Kirkpatrick, 1996)		X
(Koltin, 2013)		X
(Larson & Richburg, 2003)		X
(Latham, 2007)		X
(MacKie, 2007)		X
(McGovern, Lindemann, Vergara, Murphy, Barker, & Warrenfeltz, 2001)	X	
(Orth, Wilkinson, & Benfa, 1987)		X
(Parker, Hall, & Kram, 2008)		X
(Pearce, 2007)		X
(Petriglieri, Wood, & Petriglieri, 2011)	X	
(Popper & Lipshitz, 1992)		X
(Richards & Engle, 1986)		X
(Riddle & Ting, 2006)		X
(Sue-Chan & Latham, 2004)	X	
(Thach, 2002)	X	
(Watt, 2004)		X
(West & Milan, 2001)		X
TOTAL (48)	**12**	**36**

Table 3: Categorization of the used articles into empirical and non-empirical data

Exhibit 2

Authors	Definition of coaching
Parslow (1999)	A process that enables learning and development to occur and this performance to improve
Whitmore (1996)	Unlocking a person's potential to maximize their own performance
CIPD coaching courses definition	The overall purpose of coach-mentoring is to provide help and support for people in an increasingly competitive and pressurized world in order to help them: - develop their skills - improve their performance - maximize their potential - and to become the person they want to be
Clutterbuck (2003)	Primarily a short-term intervention aimed at performance improvement or developing a particular competence
Starr (2003)	A conversation, or series of conversations, one person has with another
Downey (1999)	The art of facilitating the performance, learning and development of another
Concise Oxford Dictionary	Defines the verb 'coach' - 'tutor, train, give hints it, prime with facts'
Caplan (2003)	A coach is a collaborative partner who works with the learner to help them achieve goals, solve problems, learn and develop
Hall et al (1999)	Meant to be a practical, goal-focused form of personal, one-on-one learning for busy executives and may be used to improve performance or executive behavior, enhance a career or prevent derailment, and work through organizational issues or chance initiatives. Essentially, coaches provide executives with feedback they would normally never get about personal, performance, career and organizational issues.
Grant (2000)	A collaborative, solution-focused, results-oriented and systematic process in which the coach facilitates the enhancement of world performance, life experience, self-directed learning and personal growth of the coach

Table 4: Definitions of coaching according to different scholars (Jarvis 2004)

Exhibit 3

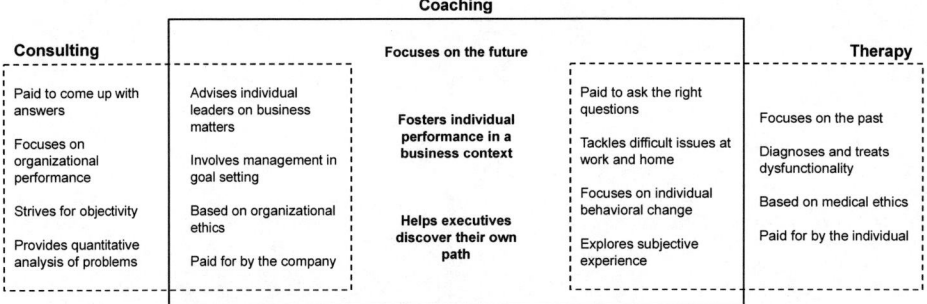

Figure 6: Delimitation of Consulting, Coaching and Therapy. (Coutu & Kauffman 2009)

Exhibit 4

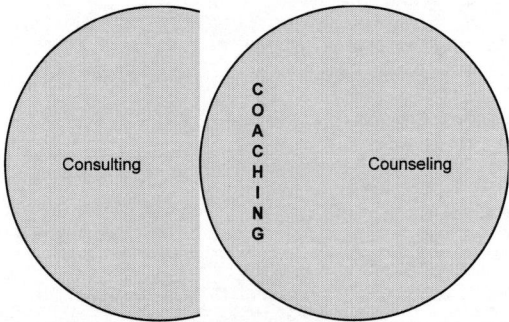

Figure 7: West and Milan Model (Bluckert 2005)

Exhibit 5

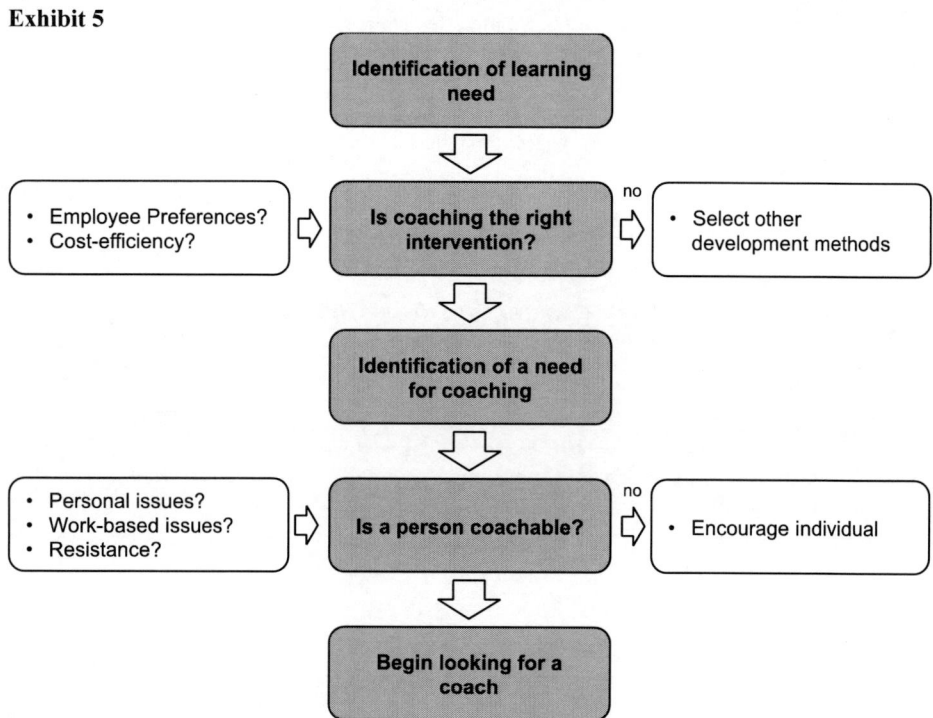

Figure 8: Process of identifying the necessity of coaching interventions (Jarvis 2004)

Exhibit 6

Authors	Leadership coaching effectiveness	Empirical Study?
Anderson (2001)	Measure of ROI: 529% return on investment	Yes, but without data published
Chiumento (2007)	96% of organizations report to have seen individual performance improve since coaching was introduced	Yes
Hall, Otazo, & Hollenbeck (1999)	Very satisfactory	No
Jarvis (2004)	92% agreed that when coaching is managed effectively it can have a positive impact on an organization's bottom line	Yes
Fielden (2005)	96% agreed coaching is an effective way to promote learning in the organization	Yes
McGovern, Lindemann, Vergara, Murphy, Barker, & Warrenfeltz (2001)	Measure of ROI: 545% return on investment	Yes

Table 5: Different attempts of scholars measuring leadership coaching effectiveness (Source: Own illustration)

Exhibit 7

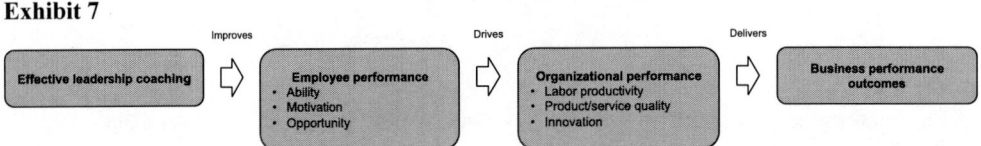

Figure 9: The result leadership coaching can have on organizations (Jarvis 2004)

References

Anderson, M. C. (2001). *Executive Briefing: Case Study on the Return on Investment of Executive Coaching.* Tampa: MetrixGlobal LLC.

Bandura, A. (1977). Social Learning Theory. *General Learning Press*, 1-46.

Barker, J. R. (1997). How can we train leaders if we don't know what leadership is? *Human Relations*, 50 (4), 343-362.

Barnett, B. G. (1995). Developing reflection and expertise: can mentors make the difference? *Journal of Educational Administration*, 33 (5), 45-59.

Berg, M. E., & Karlsen, J. T. (2012). An evaluation of management training and coaching. *Journal of Workplace Learning*, 24 (3), 177-199.

Bluckert, P. (2005). The similarities and differences between coaching and therapy. *Industrial and Commercial Training*, 37 (2), 91-96.

Bolch, M. (2001). Proactive Coaching. *Training*, 38 (5), 58-66.

Bower, K. M. (2012). Leadership Coaching: Does It Really Provide Value? *Journal of Practical Consulting*, 4 (1), 1-5.

Boyce, L. A., Jackson, J. R., & Neal, L. J. (2010). Building successful leadership coaching relationships. *Journal of Management Development*, 29 (10), 914-931.

Calkins, R. C. (1945). A challenge to business education. *Harvard Business Review*, 23 (2), 174-186.

Chiumento, S. (2007). Coaching Counts Research report 2007. London: Chiumento.

Coutu, D., & Kauffman, C. (2009). What Can Coaches Do for You? *Harvard Business Review*, 91-97.

Day, D. V., & Harrison, M. M. (2007). A multilevel, identity-based approach to leadership development. *Human Resource Management Review*, 17, 360-373.

Day, N., Surtees, J., & Winkler, V. (2008). *Learning and development: annual survey report 2008.* London: Chartered Institute of Personnel and Development.

De Meuse, K. P., & Dai, G. (2009). *THE EFFECTIVENESS OF EXECUTIVE COACHING: WHAT WE CAN LEARN FROM THE RESEARCH LITERATURE.* Los Angeles: The Korn / Ferry Institute.

Donnison, P. (2008). Executive coaching across cultural boundaries: an interesting challenge facing coaches today. *Development and learning in organizations*, 22 (4), 17-19.

Fielden, S. (2005). *Literature review: coaching effectiveness – a summary.* London: NHS Leadership Centre.

Goldsmith, M. (2012). Expanding the Value of Coaching. *The Journal for Quality & Participation*, 29-32.

Goldsmith, M. (2010). Future Leaders How can we help them? *Leadership Excellence*, 11.

Goldsmith, M., Lyons, L., Freas, A., & Witherspoon, R. (2000). *Coaching for Leadership: How the World's Greatest Coaches Help Leaders Learn.* San Francisco: Jossey-Bass.

Greene, J., & Grant, A. M. (2003). *Solution-Focused Coaching.* London: Pearson Education.

Hackman, J. R., & Wageman, R. (2007). Asking the right questions about leadership. *American Psychologist*, 62 (1), 43-47.

Hall, D. T., Otazo, K. L., & Hollenbeck, G. P. (1999). Behind Closed Doors: What Really Happens in Executive Coaching. *Organizational Dynamics*, 39-53.

Harper, S. (2012). The Leader Coach: A Model of Multi-Style Leadership. *Journal of Practical Consulting*, 4 (1), 22-31.

Hawkins, P. (2009). Developing an effective coaching strategy. *EFMD Global Focus*, 3 (3), 15-19.

Hernez-Broome, G. (2002). In It for the Long Haul: Coaching Is Key to Continued Development. *LIA*, 22 (1), 14-16.

Hogan, R., & Warrenfeltz, R. (2003). Educating the Modern Manager. *Academy of Management Learning and Education*, 2 (1), 74-84.

Hoover, J. D., Giambatista, R. C., Sorenson, R. L., & Bommer, W. H. (2010). Assessing the Effectiveness of Whole Person Learning Pedagogy in Skill Acquisition. *Academy of Management Learning & Education*, 9 (2), 192-203.

Horner, C. (2002). *Executive Coaching: The Leadership Development Tool of the Future?* London: Imperial College of Science, Technology and Medicine.

Jarvis, J. (2004). *Coaching and buying coaching services*. London: Chartered Institute of Personnel and Development.

Kegan, R., & Lahey, L. L. (2009). *Immunity to Change*. Boston: Harvard Business School Publishing Corporation.

Kets de Vries, M. (2008). *Leadership Coaching and Organizational Transformation: Effectiveness in a World of Paradoxes*. Fontainebleau: INSEAD.

Kirkpatrick, D. (1996). Great Ideas Revisited. *Training and Development*, 54-59.

Koltin, A. (2013, January). Coaching to Effect Change and Develop Talent. *CPA Practice Management Forum*, 19-21.

Larson, P. W., & Richburg, M. T. (2003). Leadership Coaching. In L. A. Berger, & D. R. Berger, *The Talent Management Handbook* (pp. 307-319). New York City: McGraw-Hill Education.

Latham, G. P. (2007). Theory and research on coaching practices. *Australian Psychologist*, 42 (4), 268-270.

Lennard, D. (2010). *Coaching Models: A Cultural Perspective*. New York: Routledge.

MacKie, D. (2007). Evaluating the effectiveness of executive coaching: Where are we now and where do we need to be? *Australian Psychologist*, 42 (4), 310-318.

McGovern, J., Lindemann, M., Vergara, M., Murphy, S., Barker, L., & Warrenfeltz, R. (2001). Maximizing the Impact of Executive Coaching: Behavioral Change, Organizational Outcomes, and Return on Investment. *The Manchester Review*, 6 (1), 1-9.

Orth, C. D., Wilkinson, H. E., & Benfa, R. C. (1987). The Managers Role as Coach and Mentor. *Organizational Dynamics*, 15 (4), 66-74.

Parker, P., Hall, D. T., & Kram, K. E. (2008). Peer Coaching: A Relational Process for Accelerating Career Learning. *Academy of Management Learning & Education*, 7 (4), 487-503.

Pearce, C. L. (2007). The future of leadership development: The importance of identity, multi-level approaches, self-leadership, physical fitness, shared leadership, networking, creativity, emotions, spirituality and on-boarding processes. *Human Resource Management Review*, 17, 355-359.

Petriglieri, G., Wood, J. D., & Petriglieri, J. L. (2011). Up Close and Personal: Building Foundations for Leaders' Development Through the Personalization of Management Learning. *Academy of Management Learning & Education*, 10 (3), 430-450.

Popper, M., & Lipshitz, R. (1992). Coaching on Leadership. *Leadership & Organization Development Journal*, 13 (7), 15-18.

Richards, D., & Engle, S. (1986). After the vision: Suggestions to corporate visionaries and vision champions. In J. D. Adams (Ed.), *Transforming Leadership* (pp.199-215). Alexandria: Miles River Press.

Riddle, D., & Ting, S. (2006). Leader Coaches Principles and Issues for In-House Development. *LIA*, 26 (2), 13-18.

Sue-Chan, C., & Latham, G. P. (2004). The relative effectiveness of external, peer, and self-coaches. *Applied Psychology: An International Review*, 53, 260-278.

Thach, E. C. (2002). The impact of executive coaching and 360° feedback on leadership effectiveness. *Leadership & Organization Development Journal*, 29 (3), 275-290.

Watt, L. (2004). Mentoring and Coaching in the Workplace . *Canadian Manager / Manager Canadien*, 14-16.

West, L., & Milan, M. (2001). *The Reflecting Glass: Professional Coaching for Leadership Development*. New York: Palgrave Macmillan.

Executive Coaching

Maren Bärenfänger, Timea Havar-Simonovich

Abstract. This article reviews current state of research and practice in the field of executive coaching. The purpose is to identify leading authors and ideas as well as polarities and research gaps by comparing existing literature contributions in the period from 2000 to 2014. The focus is on the coaching process and practices, the goals and outcomes and the final impact of executive coaching on an organization. While there is a substantial degree of agreement about the efficiency of executive coaching practices, disagree-ment is observed when considering goals and impacts. Future research is required to address the development of possible tools and techniques that enable accurate measurements of executive coaching outcome

Keywords: Coaching, training, leader, top management, CEO, organization, performance

1 Introduction

Executive coaching is a relatively new practice within global organizations (Hernez-Broome & Boyce 2011). In 2010 Business Week reported about the introduction of a new pilot program at General Motors (GE) "to bring in personal coaches for high-potential talent, a practice that GE once reserved mainly for those in need of remedial work" (Brady 2010). This illustrates the growing recognition of "on-the-job developmental relationships as important sources of managerial learning and career development" (Douglas & Morley 2000). Especially multinational Human Resource departments have already implemented executive coaching practices as a mainstream training technique to develop leadership skills (Hernez-Broome & Boyce 2011).

An annotating literature review was conducted by Douglas & Morley (2000) on behalf of the Center for Creative Leadership in North Carolina, covering the available published literature on executive coaching in the late 20th century. They searched the *Psych-Lit* as well as the *ABI-Inform* databases for articles and books referring to the specific term of "executive coaching". Articles or books that contained repeated information, that were considered poorly written or with little content were not considered in the review. As a result, they listed 49 references and summarized the main implications and concepts of each.

The purpose of this article is to summarize literature contributions on executive coaching from 2000 until the present and to identify the main fields of study together with the influential authors and their positions. Douglas & Morley (2000) identified five research gaps in their study, whose progress in current research will be analyzed. Different authors views will be contrasted and in a critical review future research gaps revealed.

2 Scholarly contributions to executive coaching between 2000 and 2014

The area of executive coaching is very dynamic, suggesting a continuous development of its definition. The executive coaching forum publishes an executive coaching handbook on a regular basis where it captures significant developments and new findings within the field. According to the 5th edition of the handbook (Ennis 2012), the following definition is considered valid:

> *"Executive coaching is an experiential and individualized leader development process that builds a leader's capability to achieve short- and long-term organizational goals. It is conducted through one-on-one and/or group interactions, driven by data from multiple perspectives, and based on mutual trust and respect. The organization, an executive, and the executive coach work in partnership to achieve maximum impact."*

McAdam (2005) provides a more simplified approach of defining executive coaching:

> *"The process by which the coach uses appropriate listening and questioning skills to work with the participant (coachee) to enable them to review and ultimately own solutions to issues upon which they seek resolution."*

These two definitions already demonstrate the variety of approaches, emerging within the theoretical and practical field of executive coaching. In reviewing the state of the literature, three main bodies of study have emerged (Douglas & Morley 2000; Kampa-Kokesch & Anderson 2008):

- *Training and development*: the coaching process and practices,
- *Psychology*: the goals and outcomes of executive coaching,
- *Management*: the impact of executive coaching on an organization.

Additionally, Douglas & Morley (2000) revealed five key research gaps concerning future theory and practice of executive coaching at the turn of millenium. They will serve as guiding questions to analyze the literature's stage of development from the year 2000 to now.

- Effectiveness of executive coaching,
- Executive coaching characteristics ensuring professional and effective interactions,
- Professional standards or guidelines for coaches and coaching processes requiring certification or licensing,
- Ethical implications of executive coaching initiatives,
- Differences to other developmental relationships such as executive consulting, mentoring, and psychotherapy.

The research gaps are assigned to each research field individually by consistence of substance. Naturally research gaps and fields overlap partially in terms of their content. Table 1 illustrates the grouping chosen for the purpose of this article.

The coaching process and practices	• Which executive coaching characteristics ensure professional and effective interactions? • Is there a need for professional standards or guidelines for coaches and coaching processes requiring certification or licensing?
The goals and outcomes of executive coaching	• Is executive coaching effective?
The impact of executive coaching on an organization	• What are ethical implications of executive coaching initiatives? • What are the differences to other developmental relationships such as executive consulting, mentoring, and psychotherapy?

Table 1: Allocation of research gaps to the study fields of executive coaching

2.1 The coaching process and practices

The first area of study addresses the coaching process, as well as common practices, and belongs to the training and developmental body of literature. Practitioners dominate the literature contributions in this area. Kilburg (2008) suggests five components that appear in every coaching process:

- Define goals, timeframe and methods,
- Build a relationship,
- Reflect coaching success and manage expectation,
- Explore choices and implement new behavior,
- Evaluate each coaching session and the coaching process' success,

This view is also supported by the five stages of executive coaching by Natale & Diamante (2005).

Another resembling approach is pursued by Stomski (2011) with his "Rapid Alignment Model", structuring the coaching process in the stages of context, contracts, coaching and evaluation.

Similar process components including claims of general validity are found in further literature contributions (Enescu & Popescu 2012; Sanson 2006; Good 2010).

Coaching methods exist countlessly. There are a wide variety of techniques offered by several coaching institutions. According to Joo (2012), most systematic approaches commonly used include "personality inventory, interviews, 360-degree feedback, and action planning". Of particular interest is the evidence for specific coaching characteristics that ensure professional and effective interactions. Bozer's (2013) empirical research suggests an improved job performance of the executive if high pre-training motivation and learning goal orientation are ensured. In contrast, the lower these characteristics, the more a negative impact on effectiveness appears. Interestingly, from the executive coaching clients' point of view, the most valued attributes of a coach are not knowledge or authenticity, but listening, understanding and encouragement (de Haan 2011). Baron & Moring (2009) identified four significant correlates to the coach-coachee relationship: the coach's self-efficacy with regard to facilitating learning and results, the coachee's motivation and perception of supervisor support, and the number of coaching sessions received.

Naturally, the question arises if there is a need for professional standards or guidelines for coaches and coaching processes requiring certification or licensing. There are many coaching guidelines offered by authors with practical experience such as the "principles for practice" proposed to coaches by McKenna & Davis (2009) or a collection of guidelines for coach and coachee summarized by the executive coaching forum (Ennis 2012). However, national or even cross-continental guidelines that ensure professional and effective coaching practices do not exist. The International Coach Federation (ICF) provides guiding principles, also adopted, for example, by Columbia University's Coaching Certification Program (Browde 2011). Additionally, the ICF offers its own certified training to coaches with awards such as "Professional Certified Coach" or "Master Certified Coach" (Sanson 2006). Future certifications requirements could be developed in alignment with existing qualifications in order to create entry barriers that secure the professionalism of executive coaching services.

2.2 The goals and outcomes of executive coaching

The second study field investigates the goals and outcomes of executive coaching, revolving around the research question whether executive coaching is effective or not. Kilburg (2008) appears again as a leading author in the here. He identified the improvement of personal and managerial competencies followed by the attempt to increase an organization's or team's effectiveness as the main goals of a coaching process. Nevertheless, more specific goals are essential to identify measures of success. These goals differ greatly among coaching projects and need to be defined between the participant and the coachee at the beginning of the coaching period (McAdam 2005).

The measurement practices of coaching effectiveness are not consistent in the coaching literature. According to Mackie (2007), there are no generally accepted criteria defining and measuring the effectiveness of executive coaching. He developed a comprehensive approach, integrating four variables influencing the coaching methodology, which in turn affects the possible outcome domains. The four variables include the coachee, the coach and the organizational characteristics as well as non-specific variables such as empathy, rapport or credibility. This approach is aimed at creating a process for a sensible comparison between various coaching results across organizations. However, it is not addressing the question if executive coaching is effective in the first place.

It is not obvious to find a vast amount of contributions with an empirical treatment of executive coaching's effectiveness. Bozer & Sarros (2012) conducted an experimental field study, analyzing the outcomes of coaching on executives' performance in terms of self-awareness, career satisfaction, job commitment, and job performance in comparison to performance without coaching. Their results suggest some performance related impact of executive coaching. However, the research was limited to Israeli coaching companies and their clients only and therefore is very restricted in terms of results transferability to other regions. More transferrable results supporting the effectiveness of executive coaching indicates the study of Moen & Skaalvik (2009) by exhibiting "significant effects of external coaching on psychological variables affecting performance such as self-efficacy, goal setting, intra-personal causal attributions of success and need satisfaction" of executives from Fortune500 companies.

Another method of defining a coaching's effectiveness is by applying the return on investment (ROI) approach. Correspondent to Atkinson's (2012) article in the journal of management services an evaluation of the current situation reveals strengths and weaknesses of the executive's attitudes, core values and behaviors at the beginning of a coaching period. However, after the coaching period it is questionable how to asses learning in terms of dollars to express the ROI, which is typically measured as (output-input)/input. Feldman & Lankau (2005) identified the self-report methodology as a very popular approach to investigate the effectiveness of executive coaching. Several studies indicate positive results in terms of effectiveness, however never expressed monetarily. Hence, intangible benefits are perceived to be the most valuable and evident outcome in the short-run, nevertheless financial gains are expected to follow (Anderson 2001). Summarized Washylyshyn (2008) suggest three indicators as measurement of a successful coaching. At first a noticeable change in sustained behavior, followed by a developed understanding and self-awareness and ultimately a more effective leadership style.

2.3 The impact of executive coaching on an organization

Specifying the impact of executive coaching on organizations' overall performance Swart & Harcup (2012) argue that by applying the 3E-model the individual learning is transferred to collective learning. 3E-model refers to three mechanisms that build up an interconnection of learning by first *enacting* behaviors, second *enacting* a coaching approach and third *embedding* collective learning processes. This implies that cognitive changes lead to behavioral changes at the individual learning level and are then followed by cognitive and behavioral changes at the collective learning level, thus enhancing the learning curve of the organization. Enescu & Popescu (2012) and Nocks (2007) even take it one step further by connecting successful organizational change to executive coaching, thereby indicating the growing need of organizations for coaching.

The competitive advantage of executive coaching against other coaching methods is not yet defined explicitly. However, for organizations it is very important to know about these differences in order to choose the most valuable method adapted to individual situations and needs. Hence, more research regarding the differences to other developmental relationships such as executive consulting, mentoring, and psychotherapy is demanded. Sanson (2006) addressed this subject matter in his dissertation and displayed the most prominent distinctions and similarities among the above mentioned coaching practices. Referring to Skiffington (2003) he concludes that executive "coaching is a synthesis of the best consulting, therapy and mentoring have to offer".

Since coaches are in a deep personal relationship with executives, ethical and moral issues may arise. However there has been very little research about ethical implications of executive coaching initiatives. An example gives Peltier (2001) by drawing attention to the confidentiality issue between coach and client. In psychotherapy it is clear that all content and even the existence of the therapy relationship are confidential. Organizations as well as individuals can be sure that even their name is kept secret. In contrast there are no global standards within the executive coaching industry, which bears potential risks to organizations (Gray 2006). In Addition to the confidentiality issue Hannafey & Vitulano (2013) submit that „potential and actual conflicts of interest, questions about professional standards, success measurement issues, and financial matters" potentially emerge due to undefined ethical foundations and moral confessions.

3 Theoretical and practical polarities in executive coaching research

Because executive coaching research is still in its infancy it is hardly surprising that many contradictory statements among various authors arise. Table 2 provides an overview of the main statements within the executive coaching area and the according authors supporting or contradicting theory.

Executive coaching practices…	Agree	Disagree
…are somehow efficient	Atkinson (2012), Bozer & Sarros (2012), Enescu & Popescu (2012), Ennis (2012), Feldman & Lankau (2005), Kilburg (2008), McAdam (2005), Nocks (2007), Sherman & Alyssa (2004), Stern (2009), Washylyshyn (2008)	–
…are somehow measurable	Anderson (2001), Atkinson (2012), Bozer & Sarros (2012), Kilburg (2008), Koonce (2010), McAdam (2005), McKenna & Davis (2009), Orenstein (2006), Washylyshyn (2008)	Joo (2012)
…are globally consistent	–	Ennis (2012), Gray (2006), Natale & Diamante (2005), Riddle, Zan & Kuzmycz (2009), Sherman & Alyssa (2004)
…have the same primary goals	McKenna & Davis (2009)	Baron & Morin (2009), Enescu & Popescu (2012), Kilburg (2008), Stern (2009)
…base on a one-on-one relationship	Baron & Morin (2009), Browde (2011), Enescu & Popescu (2012), Gray (2006), McKenna & Davis (2009), Natale & Diamante (2005)	Ennis (2012), Graham (2008), Stern (2009), Swart & Harcup (2012)
…belong to the field of psychotherapy	Bluckert (2005), Fontaine & Schmidt (2009), Graham (2008), Kilburg (2008), McKenna & Davis (2009)	Feldman & Lankau (2005), Nocks (2007), Peltier (2001), Smither (2011), Stern (2009)

Table 2: Comparison of different authors' views

4 Research gaps and future implications in the field of executive coaching

As displayed in the previous analysis most of the five research gaps identified by Douglas & Morley (2000) still demand future research. However, based on the current state of literature and the according polarities three more narrowed questions requiring further studies can be suggested:

- What measurement tools enable an effective identification of the added value resulting from executive coaching?
- What standards could be implemented in order to assure global benchmarks among executive coaches and coaching processes in professional practice?
- Is executive coaching more beneficial than alternative coaching techniques?

Researchers must compare and consolidate existing practices with implicit theories to base recommendations on achieved research results and therefore enhance executive coaching practices. The establishment of a theoretical foundation is necessary in order to reducing the risk of becoming a fading practice due to organizations perception of being costly and inefficient (Bozer 2013).

5 Conclusion

After examining the variety of research contributions evidence of two consistent messages is given. One the one hand practice application in business of executive coaching is increasing, however one the other hand empirical studies supporting this rapid growth are understudied. (Hernez-Broome & Boyce 2011). In 2004 Sherman & Alyssa stated that „no one has yet demonstrated conclusively what makes an executive coach qualified or what makes one approach to executive coaching better than another". After reviewing the current state of literature, this statement can still be considered valid. Although more evident-based as well as empirically conducted studies emerged within the last decade no comprehensive understanding about actual outcomes both on the individual and the organizational level are gained.

Executive Coaching uses a variety of approaches derived from the area of psychology, mentoring or consulting, nevertheless it is an independent field of practice mainly dealing with "healthy clients desiring a better solution or to move to a higher […] level of functioning" (Natale & Diamante 2005). Although theoretical support is lacking most executives agree on the usefulness of the coaching process in terms of removing limitations, thus becoming more effective and successful (Reeves 2006).

References

Anderson, M. C. (2001). Case Study on the Return on Investment of Executive Coaching. MetrixGlobal, LLC.

Atkinson, P. E. (2012). Return on investment in executive coaching: effective organisational change. Management Services (Spring 2012) , pp. 20-23.

Baron, L., & Morin, L. (2009). The Coach-Coachee Relationship in Executive Coaching: A Field Study. Human Ressource Development Quarterly, Spring Vol. 20/1 , pp. 85-106.

Bluckert, P. (2005). The foundations of a psychological approach to executive coaching. Industial and Commercial Training, Vol.37/4 , pp. 171-178.

Bozer, G. (2013). The role of coachee characteristics in executive coaching for effective sustainability. Journal of Management Development, Vol. 32/3 , pp. 277-294.

Bozer, G., & Sarros, J. C. (2012, February). Examining the Effectiveness of Executive Coaching on Coachees' Performance in the Israeli Context. International Journal of Evidence Based Coaching and Mentoring; 10(1) , pp. 14-32.

Brady, D. (2010, April 25). CAN GE STILL MANAGE? BusinessWeek .

Browde, B. (2011). Coaching Political Leaders: Can Coaching Be Used To Improve The Quality Of Executive-Level Government? Journal of Leadership Studies, Vol. 5/1 , pp. 71-75.

de Haan, E. (2011). Executive coaching in practice: what determines helpfulness for clients of coaching? Personnel Review, Vol. 40/1 , pp. 24-44.

Douglas, C. A., & Morley, W. H. (2000). Executive coaching: An annotated Bibliography. North Carolina: Center for Creative Leadership.

Enescu, C., & Popescu, D. M. (2012, July). Executive Coaching - Instrument for Implementing Organizational Change. Review of International Comparative Management, Vol. 13/3 , pp. 378-386.

Ennis, S. A. (2012). The Executive Coaching Handbook. Retrieved März 10, 2014, from http://www.executivecoachingforum.com/

Feldman, D. C., & Lankau, M. J. (2005, November). Executive Coaching: A Review and Agenda for Future Research. Journal of Management , pp. 828-848.

Fontaine, D., & Schmidt, G. F. (2009). The Practice of Executive Coaching Requires Practice: A Clarification and Challenge to Our Field. Industrial and Organizational Psychology, Vol. 2 , pp. 277-279.

Good, D. (2010). Cognitive Behavioral Executive Coaching. A Structure for Increasing Leader Flexibility. OD Practitioner, Vol. 42/3 , pp. 18-23.

Graham, W. (2008). Towards Executive Change: A psychodynamic group coaching model for short executive programmes. International Journal of Evidence Based Coaching and Mentoring, Vol. 6/1 , pp. 67-78.

Gray, D. E. (2006). Executive Coaching: Towards a Dynamic Alliance of Psychotherapy and Transformative Learning Processes. Management Learning, Vol. 37/4 , pp. 475-497.

Hannafey, F. T., & Vitulano, L. A. (2013). Ethics and Executive Coaching: An Agency Theory Appproach. Journal of Business Ethics , pp. 599-603.

Hernez-Broome, G., & Boyce, L. A. (2011). Advancing Executive Coaching. San Francisco: Jossey-Bass a Willey Imprint.

Joo, B.-K. e. (2012, Spring). Multiple Faces of Coaching: Manager-as-coach, Executive Coaching, and Formal Mentoring. Organization Development Journal Vol. 30/1 , pp. 19-38.

Kampa-Kokesch, S., & Anderson, M. Z. (2008). Executive coaching: A comprehensive review of the literature. In R. R. Kilburg, & R. C. Diedrich, The Wisdom of Coaching. Essential Papers in Consulting Psychology for a World of Change (pp. 39-59). Washington: American Psychological Association.

Kilburg, R. R. (2008). Toward a conceptual understanding and definition of executive coaching. In R. R. Kilburg, & R. C. Diedrich, The Wisdom of Coaching. Essential Papers in Consulting Psychology for a World of Change (pp. 21-30). Washington: American Psychological Association.

Koonce, R. (2010, September/October). Narrative 360° Assessment and Stakeholder Analysis: How a Powerful Tool Drives Executive Coaching Engagements. Global Business and Organizational Excellence , pp. 25-37.

Mackie, D. (2007, December). Evaluating the effectiveness of executive coaching: Where are we now and where do we need to be? Australian Psychologist; 42(4) , pp. 310-318.

McAdam, S. (2005). Executive Coaching: How to choose, use and maximize value for yourself and your team. London: Thorogood Publishing Limited .

McKenna, D. D., & Davis, S. L. (2009). Hidden in Plain Sight: The Active Ingredients of Executive Coaching. Industrial and Organizational Psychology, Vol.2 , pp. 244-260.

Moen, F., & Skaalvik, E. (2009). The Effect from Executive Coaching on Performance Psychology. International Journal of Evidence Based Coaching and Mentoring, Vol. 7/2 , pp. 31-49.

Murphy, S. A. (2004, November). Recourse to executive coaching: the mediating role of human resources. International Journal of Police Science & Management , pp. 175-186.

Natale, S. M., & Diamante, T. (2005). The Five Stages of Executive Coaching: Better Process Makes Better Practice. Journal of Business Ethics, Vol. 59 , pp. 361-374.

Nocks, J. (2007, April). Executive Coaching - Who Needs It? The Physician Executive , pp. 46-48.

Orenstein, R. L. (2006, Spring). Measuring Executive Coaching Efficacy? The Answer Was Here All the Time. Consulting Psychology Journal: Practice and Research, Vol 58/2 , pp. 106-116.

Peltier, B. (2001). The Psychology of Executive Coaching: Theory and Application. New York: Taylor & Francis.

Reeves, W. B. (2006, December). The Value Proposition For Executive Coaching. Financial Executive, pp. 48-49.

Riddle, D., Zan, L., & Kuzmycz, D. (2009). Five Myth About Executive Coaching. Leadership In Action: Issues & Observations, Vol. 29/5 , pp. 19-21.

Sanson, M. (2006). Executive Coaching: An international analysis of the supply of executive coaching services [Dissertation]. St. Gallen: University of St. Gallen.

Sherman, S., & Alyssa, F. (2004). The Wild West of Executive Coaching. Harvard Business Review , pp. 82-90.

Skiffington, S., & Zeus, P. (2003). Behavioral Coaching: How To Build Sustainable Personal And Organizational Strength. New South Wales: McGraw Hill.

Smither, J. W. (2011). Can Psychotherapy Research Serve as a Guide for Research About Executive Coaching? An Agenda for the Next Decade. Journal of Business Psychology, Vol. 26 , pp. 135-145.

Stern, L. R. (2009). Challenging Some Bsic Assumptions About Psychology and Executive Coaching: Who Knows Best, Who Is the Client, and What Are the Goals of Executive Coaching . Industrial and Organizational Psychology, Vol. 2 , pp. 268-271.

Stomski, L. e. (2011). Coaching Programs: Moving beyond the One-on-One. In: G. Hernez-Broome, & L. A. Boyce, Advancing Executive Coaching. Setting the Course for Successful Leadership Coaching (pp. 177-204). San Francisco: Jossey-Bass.

Swart, J., & Harcup, J. (2012). 'If I learn do we learn?': The link between executive coaching and organizational learning. Management Learning, Vol. 44/4 , pp. 337-354.

Washylyshyn, K. M. (2008). Executive Coachin: An Outcome Study. In: R. R. Kilburg, & R. C. Diedrich, The Wisddom of Coaching. Essential Papers in Consulting Psychology for a World of Change (pp. 79-89). Washington: American Psychological Association.

Team Coaching

Alyssa Mattwig, Anna Lena Theine, Debora Benson

Abstract. Teamwork becomes increasingly important owing to the fact that it enhances the outcome and team performance of a project. Team coaching is a key process that is often implemented in order to increase team performance,. Still, research about team coaching is limited. This article explores the definition, requirements, timeframe, methods, role and targets of team coaching. Therefore, various articles, journals and books have been evaluated. In order to provide a representative overview of team coaching and its functions, the scientific sources have been classified according to the authors' perspectives. Furthermore, identified research gaps are examined. This contribution reveals whether these gaps have now been addressed and identifies those research gaps for which further studies are relevant. The article concludes by stating the main features of team coaching found within the literature as well as the main differences existing in its interpretation.

Keywords: Team, team coaching, coaching, coach, team members, organization, collaboration

1 Introduction

Although both knowledge of, and theory concerning, coaching have existed for many years, team coaching gained increasing importance during the last 10-15 years (Peters & Carr 2013). This is the result of various studies which have shown that teams are more effective than individuals, because team members can share assignments, monitor behaviors, and manage different areas of each individuals' expertise (Mathieu et al. 2000) (Liu et al. 2009). Nevertheless, teams often do not work efficiently when they are negatively influenced by social, work-related or external factors. Hence, a majority of companies implement coaching to overcome these obstacles (Field 2013). A variety of literature exists that illustrates the necessity for, and definition, methods and functions of team coaching. Team coaching is a well-known term, but few experts seem to have a deeper knowledge, common understanding and appropriate approach. Hence, this article provides an overview of the topic. To illustrate the existing literature, section 2 will focus on the conducted research and its outcomes. Additionally, it describes the research gaps identified for team coaching. Further on, section 3 will provide a deeper insight into the definition and usage of team coaching. Section 4 will finally provide a conclusion on team coaching as identified in this article.

2 Conducted Research

The methodology of this paper has been conducted through secondary research via search engines and several books, which retrieved various articles. Nevertheless, many articles could not be used as they only dealt with the topic team coaching in reference to sports teams or the training of executives to become effective leaders.

Perspective	Author	Difference to other authors (if existent)
Coach will increase task performance	Fournies, 1978 Hackman, 2002 Hackman & Wageman, 2005 Peterson, 1996	
		Need tools, knowledge and opportunities provided by coach for development
Coaching will motivate	Krzyzewski, 2007 O'Hara, 2012	
Coaching attracts individual, team and organization	Anderson, Anderson & Mayo, 2008 Cox et al., 2011 Haas & vonTroschke, 2010 Kets de Vries, 2011 May, 2011 Kinlaw, 2000 Jones & Jowitt 2013	Integration and training of all for change
		Coaching can be done by everyone since it is a function and not a role
Performance shapes group relationship	Hackman, 2002 Schmid, 2005	
Coaching through a variance of modes nowadays	Payne, 2007	
Coach needs several skills	Krzyzewski, 2007 O'Hara, 2012 Young, 2006	Emotional intelligence is important, no need for expert subject knowledge
Coaching is short-term oriented	Field, 2013 Kinlaw, 2000	
		Can be short- or long-term

Figure 1: Authors' Perspective on "Coaching"

The most influential journal on team coaching and its effectiveness was written by Hackman and Wageman in 2005. The most recent research has been undertaken by Peters and Carr in 2013, which provides a good overview of the methods and implementation of team coaching. After all the sourced literature was studied, papers have been grouped according to their point of view regarding the terms coaching and team coaching in general. Figure 1 shows the established grouping referring to the term "coaching".

One can conclude that only small differences exist within the individual perspectives of "coaching". The authors agree that a coach will increase task performance and motivate, needs several skills and usually addresses the individual, team and organization as whole. Coaching exists not only through one-to-one meetings, but moreover through telephone, video conference or via email (Payne, 2007).

Young (2006) differentiates his opinion from that of Krzyzewski (2007) and O'Hara (2012) by stating that the emotional intelligence of a coach is more important than subject knowledge. Regarding the timeframe of coaching, Kinlaw (2000) sees coaching as either a short- or long-term approach whereas Field (2013) considers coaching as a short-term process only.

Perspective	Author	Difference to other authors (if existent)
Team coaching focuses on interaction not individual	Field, 2007 Hackman & Wageman, 2005 Jones & Jowitt 2013	
Team coaching focuses on task-coaching interventions	Hackman, 2002 Liu et al., 2009 Ross, 2005	Only in some situations is interpersonal coaching required
	Hackman & Wageman, 2005	Interaction with the team→success of task completion→satisfaction increases→better relationships→increased effectiveness
Focus on collective capability and performance	Clutterbuck, 2009	Underlying skills and processes (communication) not interpersonal
	Coaching at Work Ltd., 2013	Can be operated as *"skill set, practice or relationship"*
Team coaching needs reflection, analysis, motivation	Clutterbuck, 2009	

Figure 2: Authors' Perspectives on "Team coaching"

With regards to the topic of team coaching, distinctive points of view exist within the retrieved literature. The degree to which various authors' perspectives differ from one another is described in detail in section 3. Figure 2 provides an initial overview of the differences existing within the definition of the term "team coaching". Overall we can say that team coaching is a method to increase the task performance of a team and a collective interaction that needs inward reflection and motivation provided by the coach.

Although much literature has been written about team coaching in a wider sense, it is still not a deeply researched topic. Examining the sourced journal articles and books, the following research gaps were identified:

	Identified by	Further research	Result
Literature focuses on skill-acquisition	Fournies, 1978	Goldberg, 2003 Hackman & Wageman, 2005 Reich et al., 2009	- Functions that coaches serve - Identification of specific time for team coaching - Conditions under which team coaching facilitates performance
Lack of research beyond coaching for task-performance	Hackman & Wageman, 2005		
Little research about the effect of team coaching for team effectiveness	Hackman & Wageman, 2005		
Little guidance exists for managers and team leaders	Jones & Jowitt, 2013		
Little guidance exists for implementation of specific team coaching methods	Cox, 2013 Peters & Carr, 2013	Field, 2007 Groß, n.d Hawkins, 2011 Kets de Vries, 2011 Ross, 2005	Various methods
Lack of research beyond athletic coaching and executive coaching	Liu et al., 2009	Liu et al., 2009	Research within a specific team in Taiwan

Figure 3: Research gaps

The first research gap reveals that team coaching focuses mainly on acquisition of new skills by team members (Fournies 1978). Hackman and Wageman (2005) showed further that team coaching often deals with task-performance of teams and limited research exists about its effectiveness on teams. Following on, they researched the functions that coaches serve, identified specific time periods for coaching and conditions under which team coaching facilitates performance (Hackman & Wageman 2005). Nevertheless, only the studies by Hackman & Wageman (2005) and by Reich et al. (2009) deal with the effect of team coaching on a team. Furthermore, Hackman & Wageman (2005) focus on their interpretation of team coaching which is increasing the task performance of a team. Little guidance exists for managers and team leaders on how they can become a coach for their employees (Jones & Jowitt 2013). Additionally, limited guidance exists for the implementation of specific methods (Peters & Carr 2013). Moreover, most literature on team coaching refers to athletic or executive coaching but there has been relatively little research on team coaching in a business context for every employee (Liu et al. 2009).

3 Team Coaching

The following section addresses the definition of team coaching, its requirements, the best time for implementing team coaching, delivery methods and the role of the coach, in addition to overall targets.

3.1 Definition

Team coaching was defined by Hackman and Wageman (2005) as "direct interaction with a team intended to help members make coordinated and task-appropriate use of their collective resources in accomplishing the team's work" (p.269). Distinct from one-to-one coaching, team coaching focuses on the direct interaction with the team as whole and not the development of individual members (Field 2007); (Hackman & Wageman 2005); (Jones & Jowitt 2013); (Landsiedel NLP Training 2014). Moreover, many articles reveal that coaching should always address the individual, the team and the organization similarly, in order to increase the positive outcome of coaching (Kinlaw 2000); (Anderson et al. 2008); (Jones & Jowitt 2013); (Kets de Vries 2011); (Cox et al. 2011); (Haas & von Troschke 2010); (May 2011). Moreover, coaching can identify mechanisms to increase organizational growth and development (Rosha 2014). While coaching is often seen as a personal development option for the coachee, team coaching focuses on improving the task-performance of a team (Ross 2005); (Hackman 2002); (Liu et al. 2009); (Hackman & Wageman 2005); (Clutterbuck 2009). Explicitly, Ross (2005) highlights that only in certain situations, is interpersonal coaching necessary. Hackman and Wageman (2005) see a self-influencing mechanism between relationship and task-oriented team coaching: Interaction with the team leads to the success of completing a task, which increases satisfaction, which in turn creates better relationships that increase a team's effectiveness. Clutterbuck, however (2009) puts emphasis on collective capability and performance during team coaching. Collective capability, Clutterbuck (2009) defines as underlying skills and processes, such as communication skills, and not interpersonal relationship building. Nevertheless, no common definition for coaching and team coaching exist (Ladyshewsky 2010); (Passmore & Fillery-Travis 2011).

3.2 Requirements

NLP, the neuro-linguistic programming theory, differentiates between internal and external issues that team coaching can solve. Internal issues refer to ambiguous team tasks, roles of team members or sympathy and antipathy between the team members. On the other hand, if the client/boss relationship is not binding enough, conflicts across other teams and communication difficulties with customers will exist, These are seen as external issues (Landsiedel NLP Training 2014). In order to overcome these issues and implement team coaching successfully, the team should exhibit certain characteristics. Hawkins (2011) states the following characteristics, which have been identified by Tichy and Devanna (1986) for transformational leaders, as a basis for transformational leadership teams. Since every team has to follow a change process during team coaching interventions, these characteristics can be seen as requirements for every team: Team members should see themselves as change agents and be courageous. It is of further importance that all members believe in good and willing people. The team must be driven by a strong set of values. Likewise, team members should have a tendency to be lifelong learners, which will make the implementation for change easier for the coach. The team should be willing to cope with complexity, uncertainty and ambiguity. Lastly, team coaching can be more successful if team members are visionaries (Hawkins 2011). To understand more about the team, members must first be aware of their own behavior within the team. Once members know their own needs and working style, they can be more aware of the interaction with their team members. Hence, team members can understand others, adapt to them and bring in their own perspectives more efficiently. As a result, engagement and creativity can be increased while conflicts can be decreased (Jones & Jowitt 2013). On the subject of organizational circumstances, for effectiveness, key processes of a team must be unconstrained from task or organizational structures. Furthermore, the team must be well designed and the organizational context supportive of team work. Concerning coaching, interventions should only be implemented when a team is ready for them (Hackman 2002); (Hackman & Wageman 2005).

3.3 Time for Implementation

Coaching occurs *"when words of encouragement are being offered"* (Kinlaw 2000 p.38). It can be done by anyone, such as internal or external managers and consultants, at any point of time (Hackman 2002). Hence, it may occur collectively, e.g. during team meetings, or through one-to-one interactions, usually between the team leader and a team member (Liu et al. 2009). According to Hawkins (2011), coaching for teams depends on the teams' need for intervention, varying from minor course corrections to top-to-bottom overhaul. Little research exists about the right time for applying team coaching. Peters and Carr (2013) in addition to Hackman and Wageman (2005) agree that the most effective times for implementing team coaching are exactly during the beginning, midpoint and end-stage of a team's lifecycle. At the beginning stage, a team may be newly established or an existing team may be confronted with a new project, strategy, initiative, fiscal year or business cycle (Peters & Carr 2013). At this point, motivational coaching to increase a team's effort is most useful (Hackman & Wageman 2005); (Hackman 2002). This can be done by creating the appropriate conditions to assess, design and launch a team. Ongoing team and peer coaching should be established during this phase. In general, team coaching is most effective during the beginning-stage as it affects all further processes of a teams' lifecycle. Throughout the midpoint of a team's project, a team might want to rethink its strategy, process or project behavior (Peters & Carr 2013). Thus, consultative coaching that concentrates on the performance strategy should be used (Hackman & Wageman 2005); (Hackman 2002). Team coaching is more difficult during this stage, although team members want and need review during this time. It is important for the coach to focus on the team's learning opportunities and to define a team strategy (Peters & Carr 2013). After a project has been completed (end-stage), educational coaching should be implemented to put emphasis on knowledge and skills gained during the project (Hackman 2002). However, team coaching is also helpful in between those stages and can be used to reinforce effectiveness and coordinate activities (Hackman & Wageman 2005). Moreover, it should be seen as a process and not as a one-time intervention (Haas & von Troschke 2010).

3.4 Methods

Team coaching is seen as a valuable tool nowadays, but no accepted method and view exists on how to successfully implement it in organizations. Some articles revealed questions on how the team can achieve goals or personality factors and tips for dealing with failure that occur within a team (Payne, 2007); (Ross 2005). By contrast, other authors recommended tools, such as a team development survey, the Myers-Briggs type indicator, Tuckman's model, a two-day long program or the Streitberg-process (Field 2007); (Ashauer 2011); (Ross 2005); (Groß n.d.). Kets de Vries is one of the few who proposes two-day long team coaching training, according to Ross (2005). After an initial discussion about effective leadership and characteristics of high performance teams, personal feedback is provided by the coach. During the second day, the personal feedback is shared with the group to develop objectives for each team member. This increases trust, honesty and openness. After a couple of months, he proposes a follow-up session held by the coach to outline the progress achieved (Ross 2005). Similarly, a team also runs through three phases during the Streitberg-process. Within the first phase, if all members accept each individual as they currently stand, the individual can recognize his potential, develop it, and implement it (Groß n.d.). Continuing the process, the team commits itself toward common means and takes a deeper insight into the company's leadership style, management system, trends and organizational structure (phase of ability). Here, Groß (n.d.) is in agreement with the majority of other authors who see team coaching as necessary for improving the interaction of individuals, teams and the organization (Anderson et al. 2008); (Kinlaw 2000); (Jones & Jowitt 2013). During the third phase, common ways of acting are learned, trained and consolidated, e.g. by working on a specific topic to experience common planning and actions (Groß n.d.). Regardless of the applied method, at the end of the team coaching process, an action plan should show the task of each individual to fulfill the team change. Within this plan, each member should have a stake in someone else's goal to ensure a common identity (Kets de Vries 2011). Acknowledging the fact that more research has been conducted on team coaching for sports teams, a toolkit was developed by the Financial & Legal Skills Partnership, in 2013. The experiences of six key sport coaches have been taken and transformed into a business context. It is intended to encourage managers to become good coaches for their teams by increasing a positive environment, motivation and development possibilities for their employees (Field 2013). All these methods cannot be used if a team does not keep certain aspects in mind according to Krüger (2008), cited by Haas & von Troschke (2010). The interest of every person has to be considered harmoniously. Furthermore, distinct and accepted goals have to be defined and teamwork has to be seen as priority. This increases the commitment toward meetings and milestones. Internal concurrence has to be overcome while improving communication within the team. Lastly, group loyalty should be increased by the team leader (Haas & von Troschke 2010).

3.5 Role of the Coach

With the aim being to deliver successful team coaching interventions, a coach should have certain character traits. The following traits can be determined in reference to several articles and books: Influencing, patient, open-minded, reflective, respectful, flexible, trustworthy, appreciative, and knowledgeable and experienced about team processes.

According to these characteristics, a team coach should facilitate collaborative team problem solving, provide feedback and advise a team on how to work effectively (internally and with other teams) (Kets de Vries 2011); (Kinlaw 2000); (Clutterbuck 2009); (Payne, 2007); (Haas & von Troschke 2010). Moreover, the coach should encourage support of the members for the team and teach interpersonal skills. It is of importance that the coach is always present during essential meetings to observe the team structure and performance. Nonetheless, a team coach is only a guide for the team and should not serve as a solution-provider (Kets de Vries 2011); (Kinlaw 2000); (Payne, 2007).

Hawkins CID-CLEAR model outlines, in eight steps, the tasks and role of a coach (Hawkins 2011 p.67-82):

1. *"Contracting through initial exploratory discussions*
2. *Inquiry or establishing real world data on team*
3. *Diagnosis and design*
4. *Contracting the outcomes and ways of working*
5. *Listening*
6. *Exploration and experiment*
7. *Action*
8. *Review"*

This process helps coaches to stay on track during the team coaching process. As can be seen from the outlined characteristics and the CID-CLEAR model, the coach only intervenes as a guide, and after he has understood the team process. Hence, responsibility can be taken on by the team members to increase team capability. Last but not least, the team coach helps a team to clarify actions and expected results from each member. The tasks and delivery dates rely on the teams decisions (Payne, 2007).

3.6 Targets

Some authors of the reviewed literature agree that team coaching improves team performance, effectiveness and collective actions (Ross 2005); (Hackman & Wageman 2005); (Groß n.d.); (Liu et al. 2009). In contrast, Clutterbuck (2009) states a positive effect for the individuals of a team. Team coaching underlines the personal development of individuals, their performance and faced barriers (Clutterbuck 2009). A further perspective, gained within a Taiwanese study, exposed positive effects for the team members effort, skills and knowledge, but retrieved no correlation with the implementation of a strategy for successful task performance (Liu et al. 2009). However, many authors agreed, if a team leader takes the position of a coach, he can increase a positive attitude of employees by providing training, development plans and feedback (Field 2013); (Clutterbuck 2009); (Ellinger et al. 2011). Coaches observed that coaching has the greatest impact on the relationships and teamwork among employees of different levels within an organization (Rosha 2014). Nevertheless, only continuous improvement helps teams to achieve their full potential (Payne, 2007).

4 Conclusion

This article outlines that team coaching is a topic with many diverse opinions and approaches. Additionally, empirical evidence is lacking that reveals the effectiveness of team coaching. Although many tools are provided for the process of team coaching, little evidence of a positive effectiveness might represent a barrier for organizations. Coaching itself is not a standardized process. It always depends on the team, its individuals and the environment. Hence, authors cannot be easily grouped. Nevertheless, the majority of the reviewed literature agrees that team coaching is not a method to overcome interpersonal misunderstandings, but focuses on the task the team has to fulfill successfully.

Team coaching has no limitation regarding team size and effects on an organization's culture and profitability. Team members must be willing to change and support each other during the coaching process. Team coaching is most successful at the beginning-stage of a team process. In order to implement team coaching, several methods, such as the Streitberg-process, can be used. Although many methods have been established, little research exists about their effectiveness. This research gap has yet to be closed. Furthermore, this article highlights that a team coach is a guide during the coaching process. Interfering as a problem-solver might decrease a feeling of belongingness for the team members.

Although team coaching gains importance, it lacks an agreed definition, deeper knowledge of experts and long-term studies about the effectiveness for organizations. It is considered difficult for a "new" coach to be a good supporter for a struggling team. Also, some research gaps, such as little guidance in the business context, are still not fully evaluated. Team coaching will always be a subjective intervention that depends on the coach and the team itself. Here, a well-defined process will reduce an effective outcome and would leave no room for adaptation where it is needed the most.

References

Anderson, M. C.; Anderson, D. L.; Mayo, W. D. (2008). Team Coaching Helps a Leadership Team Drive Cultural Change at Caterpillar. *Global Business & Organizational Excellence*. 27(4). p. 40-50.

Ashauer, S. (2011). Group and Team Coaching: The Essential Guide by Christine Thornton. *Personnel Psychology*. 64(4). p. 1059-1063.

Buchner, D. (1995). Team-Coaching: Gemeinsam zum Erfolg. Wiesbaden: Gabler Verlag.

Clutterbuck, D. (2009). Coaching teams in the workplace. *Global Focus: The EFMD Business Magazine*. 3(3). p. 9-14.

Coaching at Work Ltd. (2013). Team coaching: systemic approach is 'vital'. *Coaching at Work*. 8(1). p. 8.

Cox, E. (2013). *Coaching Understood: A Pragmatic Inquiry into the Coaching Process*. London, California, New Delhi, Singapore: Sage Publications Ltd.

Cox, E., Bachkirova, T., Clutterbuck, D. (2011). *The Complete Handbook of Coaching*. Los Angeles, California, London: Sage Publications Ltd.

Ellinger, A., Beattie, R.; Halmin, R. (2011). The Manager as 'Coach'. In: E. Cox, T. Bachkirova & D. Clutterbuck. *The Complete Handbook of Coaching*. London, California, New Delhi, Singapore: Sage Publications Ltd.

Field, A. (2007). Coaching Your Team's Performance to the Next Level: How team coaching can reduce conflict and increase collaboration-and hence a team's productivity. *Harvard Management Update*. 12(11). p. 3-5.

Field, L. (2013). *Enhanced team performance through effective management coaching*. Money Marketing (Online Edition). available from http://www.moneymarketing.co.uk/news-and-analysis/advisers/liz-field-enhanced-team-performance-through-effective-management-coaching/2000139.article, reviewed 02-06-2014.

Fournies, F. F. (1978). *Coaching for improved work performance*. Bridgewater, NJ: Van Nostrand Reinhold.

Golderbg, S. (2003). Team Effectiveness Coaching: An Innovative Approach for Supporting Teams in Complex Systems. *Leadership & Management in Engineering*. 3(1). p. 15.

Groß, J. (n.d.). Teamcoaching vs. Gruppen-Coaching. *Coaching-magazin* (Online Edition). available from http://www.gross-team.com/docs/Coaching_Magazin.pdf, reviewed 02-07-2014.

Guzzo, R. A., Dickson, M. W. (1996). Teams in organisations: Recent research on performance and effectiveness. *Annual Review of Psychology*. 47. p. 307-338.

Haas, B., von Troschke, B. (2010). *Teamcoaching: Exzellenz vom Zufall Befreien*. Wiesbaden: Gabler Verlag / Springer Fachmedien Wiesbaden GmbH.

Hackman, J. R. (2002). *Leading Teams: Setting the stage for great performances*. Boston, Massachusetts: Harvard Business School Press.

Hackman, J. R.; Wageman, R. (2005). *A Theory of Team Coaching*. Academy of Management Review. 30(2). p. 269-287.

Hawkins, P. (2011). *Leadership Team Coaching: Developing Collective Transformational Leadership*. London, UK, Philadelphia, PA: Kogan Page Limited.

Jones, P., Jowitt, A. (2013). Coaching the team. *Training Journal*, p. 64-69.

Katzenbach, J. R., Smith, D. K. (1993). The discipline of teams. *Harvard Business Review*. 71(2). p. 111-120.

Kets de Vries, M. F. R. (2011). *The Hedgehog Effect: The Secrets of Building High Performance Teams.* West-Sussex: John Wiley & Sons.

Kinlaw, D. C. (2000). Encourage Superior Performance from People and Teams Through Coaching. *Women in Business*. 52(1). p. 38-41.

Krzyzewski, M. (2007). Coaching Teams: Know Your Talent. *Personal Excellence*. 12(8). p. 15.

Ladyshewsky, R. (2010). The manager as coach as a driver of organizational development. *Leadership & Organization Development Journal*. 31(4). p. 292-306.

Landsiedel NLP Training. (2014). *Teamcoaching.* available from http://www.landsiedel-seminare.de/coaching-bibliothek/teamcoaching/methoden.html, reviewed 02-06-2014.

Liu, C.-Y., Pirola-Merlo, A.; Yang, C.-A., Huang, C. (2009). Disseminating the Functions of Team Coaching Regarding Research and Development Team Effectiveness: Evidence from High-Tech Industries in Taiwan. *Social Behavior & Personality: An International Journal*. 37(1). p. 41-57.

Mathieu, J. E., Heffner, T. S., Goodwin, G. F., Salas, E., Cannon-Bowers, J. A. (2000). The influence of shared mental models on team process and performance. *Journal of Applied Psychology*. 85. p. 273–283.

May, K. (2011). Coach employees for winning teams. Communication Briefings. 2. p. 2.

O'Hara, K. (2012). Coaching your team: How any executive can become a better mentor and coach to high potential employees. *Smart Business Orange County*. 6(12). p. 24.

Passmore, J., Fillery-Travis, A.(2011). A critical review of executive coaching research: a decade of progress and what's to come. *Coaching: An international journal of theory, research and practice*. 4(2). p. 70-88.

Payne, V. (2007). Chapter 7: Coaching Teams for High Performance. In Coaching for High Performance. p. 115-133. New York: American Management Association International.

Peters, J., Carr, C. (2013). *High Performance Team Coaching*. Canada: Friesen Press.

Peterson, D. B. (1996). Executive coach at work: The art of one-on-one change. *Consulting Psychology Journal*. 48. p. 78-86.

Reich, Y., Ullmann, G., van der Loos, M., Leifer, L. (2009). Coaching product development teams: A conceptual foundation for empirical studies. *Research in Engineering Design*. 19(4). p. 205-222.

Rosha, A. (2014). *Peculiarities of manifestation of coaching in organisations*. Procedia - Social and Behavioral Sciences. 110. p. 852–860.

Ross, J. A. (2005). How to Be the Best Coach for Your Team: Should you focus on relationships or tasks? Here's how to decide. *Harvard Management Update*. 10(11). p. 3-5.

Schmid, B. (2005). *Coaching und Team-Coaching aus systemischer Perspektive*. available from http://www.systemische-professionalitaet.de/download/schriften/97-coaching-und-team-coaching-aus-systemischer-perspektive.pdf, reviewed 02-06-2014.

Section III: Organizational Interventions

Organizational Consulting

Corinna Horn, Lisa Molitor

Abstract. This article serves to explore 'organizational consulting' in order to better understand its purpose, approaches as well as origin. A range of published works beginning in the early 20th century up to today have been reviewed. The sources are sorted into sections: introduction to consulting, origin and history, concepts, process models, roles of consultants, approaches, conclusion, state of the art and research gaps. Consulting, with its long history, underwent several turning points and additionally has been influenced by certain other research areas, such as organizational development. Consulting occupies a significant role in modern organizations and can be seen as an economic activity. Furthermore, consultants can be perceived as promoters of organizational and societal change. Nevertheless, there are several underexplored and truly unexplored areas of consulting.

Keywords: Organizational consulting, consulting, management consulting, consulting industry, management studies, organizational change, IT consulting, knowledge management

1 Introduction

Organizational consulting can be defined as "a professional service that assists businesses in evaluating and possibly restructuring the current internal layout of the company" (Tatum 2014). Commonly, organizational consulting is simply referred to as 'consulting' and has been used with a variety of denotations (Biswas & Twitchell 2002: 6; Day 2004: 27; von Keller & Lorentz 1999: 349-351; Ziegler 1995; Graubner 2007) Furthermore, management consulting falls under the umbrella term consulting as well and there are several notions that vary with culture and language (Hofmann et al. 1991; Kipping & Armbruester 1999; Kubr 2002; Wohlgemuth 1995; Graubner 2007). Therefore, 'management consulting' and 'consulting' are used interchangeably in this article. This article will focus on the origins and history of consulting, the dominant themes that have been established as well as several approaches.

Due to the fact that research on management consulting "has found it difficult to meet the two most important conditions for publication in the top-rated management journals in North America: the need to contribute to a major theoretical concern and to collect systematic, ideally quantitative data as the basis for statistical analysis and hypothesis testing" (Kipping & Clark 2012), most consulting publications have been articles in the business press, in specialist literature and in textbooks.

2 Consulting

First, consulting is defined and the next section deals with the origins and history of consulting while the following sections discuss the consulting concept and process as well as the role of a consultant.

Consulting plays an ever growing role in todays organizations, dispersed amongst different conceptual approaches and disciplines. Consulting research is an interdisciplinary endeavor and presents a method into several critical issues that have engaged social science for more than fifty years. "These issues include the shifting nature of organizations, the rise of management, the nature of knowledge, professions, fashion, and the post-industrial economy" (Kipping & Clark 2012). Regardless of the characteristic periodic structural shifts in the consulting industry, at its core, it is an advisory activity based on the relationship between client and consultant (Kipping & Clark 2012).

2.1 Origins and History of Consulting

Frederick Winslow Taylor is referred to as the "Father of Scientific Management"; according to Taylorists, his "concept combined the practice of engineering with the principles of economics, and it was out of this coupling that today's profession was born" (McKenna). A contrary assumption is that the origins of modern management consulting are in the 1930s and Taylorism was not the predominant influence on the development of consulting firms (McKenna). "Rather, management engineers drew on the practices of accountants, engineers, and lawyers to offer CEO-level studies of organization, strategy, and operations" (McKenna).

Before and during World War II, literature regarding consulting was exclusively limited to a few articles in business and the general press. The first broad overview of the consulting industry and its activities can be found in the book 'The Business Healers' (Higdon 1969). While most early publications were written by journalists, later publications were from consultants themselves. The majority of books authored by these 'early' consultants are mere summaries of consultants ideas rather than reflections on the industries activities (Kipping & Clark 2012). One exception is C. B. Thompson the author of 'The Theory and Practice of Scientific Management' (1917) who examined "the implementation and effects of the diverse systems as well as the reactions of those concerned" (Kipping & Clark 2012:12). "Another stream of academic research concerned with consulting comes form the literature on organizational development" (McKenna). Schein (1969) identified the distinctiveness of an "organizational development practitioner as a process consultant" (McKenna). What unites most authors prior to 1975 is a generally positive attitude towards consultancy and their believe that when correctly applied consulting can make a difference. From the mid-1970s onwards, this was to change and a broadening of the approaches towards the industry could be observed (McKenna). Over the years, rather than focusing on consulting activities, numerous comparative studies of the different systems of scientific management were published. Finally, in the 1980s, the labor process theory recognized the roles of consultants (McKenna). Originally a Marxist message, it was widely entertained in British business schools (Rowlinson & Hassard 2001).

The often mentioned starting point for management bestsellers authored by celebrity consultants is 'In Search of Excellence' (Peters and Waterman 1982) (Kipping & Clark 2012). Other literature published during this decade broadly addressed consulting firms and their activities. Academic attention was gained by management consulting as well as focus was continued on organizational development with influential updated editions (e.g. French & Bell 1995). Moreover, work on organizational development "branched out into a much more normative literature, which tried to provide guidelines and advice for those wanting to offer consultancy services" (Kipping & Clark 2012). Likewise, an increasing number of publications provided an insight to the work of consultants to its readers, specifically managers and management students (e.g. Biech 1999; Rasiel 2001). "Others, recognizing the rise of knowledge-intensive firms, developed titles specifically focusing on how to manage these firms (e.g. Maister 1993)" (Kipping & Clark 2012:15). As the consulting industry grew unprecedented since the 1990s, so did the academic research and even more so accounts of management consulting, particularly as an economic function. Furthermore, publishers during this research boom have taken a mostly critical perspective towards the consulting industry and its activities (Kipping & Clark 2012). With the academic research, an increasing demand in management consulting courses arose and subsequently, numerous dedicated textbooks have been published. Noteworthy are Wickham (1999), Biswas & Twitchell (2001). Unfortunately, despite the success of the textbooks in terms of sales, with the exception of O'Mahoney's (2010) textbook, these textbooks contain little if any actual research (Kipping & Clark 2012). The single most comprehensive contribution to the literature from a practical perspective according to Kubr (2002) up to today is 'Management Consulting: A Guide to the Profession' published by the International Labour Office in 1976.

During the 1990s, particularly due to scholarly interest, critical views became louder when studies examined consulting from a labor perspective. Intrinsically, these studies analyzed the contribution of consultants to the degradations of workers. "The most comprehensive work of this kind was conducted by Littler (1982). [...] Consulting received even greater academic attention as labour process theory morphed into critical management studies, where the focus extended beyond the politics of work organization and capitalism into a more general critique of managerialism, hegemony, and power" (Kipping & Clark 2012). Another focus was on 'neo-institutionalism' in management and organization theory. DiMaggio & Powell (1983:152) highlight in their article, which became a 'manifesto of neo-institutionalism', that "large organizations choose from a relatively small set of major consulting firms, [...] which spread a few organizational models throughout the land" (Kipping & Clark 2012). "Unlike labour process theory, this was a more neutral view, which is why it was eventually questioned by more critical scholars and those seeing a translation rather than transmission process at work" (Kipping & Clark 2012).

Also during the 1990s, some authors have critically "investigated the rhetorical techniques used by management consultants and gurus […] others have stressed the legitimizing role of consultants in internal conflicts and with respect to external stakeholders (Jackall 1988; Faust 2000; Kipping 2000). A number of popular books have gone even further, highlighting the potential dangers of hiring consultants and identifying the tricks they use to gain and retain clients (O'Shea & Madigan 1997; Ashford 1998; cf. also Argyris 2000). This rather negative evaluation of consultants stands in clear contrast to the earlier, much more positive literature, which compared consultants to medical doctors (Higdon 1969) or made efforts to understand and categorize their roles in organizational development (e.g. Schein 1988)" (Kipping & Engwall 2002).

2.2 Consulting Concepts

As consultants observe, analyze their findings in the context of theory, and draw conclusions they can be thought of as the academics of the business world (Szczerba 2013). Hence, consultants utilize theoretical concepts. The BCG Matrix is probably the most famous theoretical concept. It was developed by the Boston Consulting Group in 1968 and published by the Harvard Business Review (Ovans 2011). The purpose of the tool is to assist companies to allocate its resources. Another tool designed by the Boston Consulting Group (1960) is the experience curve. "The theory states that there is an inverse relationship between production and costs: each time production volume doubles, cost fall by a constant percentage' (Szczerba 2013).

"Developed by Harvard Business School Professor Michael Porter, Porter's Five Forces is a framework that determines how profitable an industry could be for its players and where and how within it a company might have room to compete"

(Szczerba 2013). The last concept is 'core competencies', a concept devised by CK Prahalad and Gary Hamel from the University of Michigan. "The key idea is that each business has a 'core competency', a factor that's central to the way in which it or its employees work" (Szczerba 2013).

"Leavitt (1962) suggested that organizations could be developed or changed by altering one or more of three major variables - people, structure and technology. "Peters and Waterman (1982) widened the range of variables in their adoption of a seven-item framework" known as the McKinsey 7-S framework and published it in their book 'In Search of Excellence' (Shodhganga). The 7-S concept is also a widely utilized tool by consultants.

2.3 Consulting Process Models

Process complexity and the required process know-how determines which consulting process model is utilized. The three basic models most commonly used are the problem solving model developed by Schein (1987), the process moderation model described by G. Lippitt & R. Lippitt (1986) as well as by P. H. Block in 'Flawless Consulting' (2000) and the systemic consulting model also called the 'systemic loop' by Koenigswieser & Hillebrand (2005). Kubr describes the standardized phases of the consulting process in his reference work "Management Consulting : A Guide to the Profession" as follows: entry, diagnosis, action planning, implementation and termination.

2.4 Roles of Consultants

G. Lippitt & R. Lippitt present in their bestselling book 'The Consulting Process in Action' (1986) a framework describing the (8) roles of a consultant, namely: objective observer, process counselor, fact finder, identifier of alternatives and linker to resources, joint problem solver, trainer/educator, information specialist and advocate. For many consultants and managers this book has served as reference work for many years. Another approach to the roles of consultants has been put forward by revered author E. H. Schein (1987), he identified three roles of consultants - the expert role, pair-of-hands role and the collaborative role - and additionally analyzed their respective activities. Block perceives consultants as providers of practical advice and help rather than a professional service (Kubr 2002). "The role of the consultant also has a bearing on the decision about what outcomes will be sought and measured. Some consulting firms do analysis and recommendations only […], other consultants are more focused on how to implement the changes the organization desires" (Winum & Nielsen & Bradford).

3 Consulting Approaches

Different academic disciplines have contributed to consulting research. "Sociology - as well as management and organization studies based on sociological approaches - and economics present the opposite ends of the spectrum […] (Armbruester 2006)" (Kipping & Clark 2012).

M. Kipping and T. Clark describe the consulting industry in their reference work 'The Oxford Handbook of Management Consulting' as proven to be very adaptable, "as it has sought to sustain demand for its services in a context that, occasionally, radically alters". Out of this constant state of change, several disciplinary and inter-disciplinary approaches have developed. Inter-disciplinary approaches are increasingly implemented. One of the most widely used approaches in consulting is organizational development (OD) which stems from techniques originally used by behavioral scientists. It "applies behavioral-science knowledge and practices to help organizations change to achieve greater effectiveness. It seeks to improve how organizations relate to their external environments and function internally to attain high performance and high quality of work life. It is both an applied field of social practice and a domain of scientific inquiry. Although several definitions of OD have been presented by different philosophers like Beckhard (1969), Bennis (1966), French (1969), Burke (1982), Beer (1980), French & Bell (1990), Schein (1992), Luthans (1998), Robbins (2003), Ogundele (2005), Armstrong (2006), etc., yet enormous growth of new approaches and techniques has blurred the boundaries of the field and made it increasingly difficult to de-scribe" (Cummings & Worley 2009).

Another approach to consulting is the 'Tavistock tradition'. "This 'tradition' seeks to bring together insights from psychoanalysis, group relations, and open systems theory, to understand and address organizational dilemmas, challenges, and discontents [...]. Recently it has come to be referred to as 'system psychodynamics' (Gould, Stapley & Stein 2001; Neumann 1999)" (Armstrong 2005). A related approach and specialty area of psychology is the field of organizational consulting psychology, which "is based on science, but mostly about translating science into practice [...] as it combines the discipline of theory building with the reality of practice" (Lowman 2003).

Furthermore, another approach also related to the field of psychology is the 'Gestalt Approach' to organizational consulting. Gestalt therapy has developed in the 1940s (Perls 1947; Perls et al. 1951). "This approach derived largely out of an attempt to integrate into psychoanalytic theory the findings of the Gestalt studies of perception and learning by Wertheimer (1945), Koffka (1922, 1935), and Kohler (1927, 1929, 1947); the related work of Kurt Lewin (1935, 1951a) and Kurt Goldstein (1939); and work by other phenomeno-logical and existential thinkers. Gestalt consulting involves an active, strong presence on the part of the consultant" (Nevis 2013).

4 Conclusion

Consulting has managed to occupy a significant role in modern organizations in a relatively short period of time. "Today, consultants are ubiquitous in the business world and even beyond their advisory role" (Kipping & Clark 2012). More attention is being paid to consulting for several reasons: consulting can be seen as an economic activity, for the human resources it employs and consultants can be perceived as promoters of organizational (and societal) change (Kipping & Clark 2012).

4.1 State of the Art

Over the past two decades interest in and the publications – by journalists and consultants – on consulting increased. Particularly after the Enron scandal, criticism of the industry became louder. Nevertheless, academic research also increased and came into its own. Many researchers also adopted a rather critical view (Clark & Fincham 2002). Work by Abrahamson (esp. 1991, 1996, 2011) in particular is worth mentioning as he drew the "attention of researchers towards the notion of 'management fashions' and of 'fashion-setting communities', and how the latter, which include [...] consultancies, produce ideas to be consumed by managers" (Kipping & Clark 2012). "However, much of the research and the subsequent publications [...] emanated from Europe and were published in European-based journals [...]. This is all the more surprising as the industry itself originated in the United States, where it continues to have its largest market today (Wright & Kipping; McKenna 2006; Kipping 2012)" (Kipping & Clark 2012). The reason for this is quite likely the same as to why the two most important conditions for publications in top-rated management journals in North America are not met (see introduction). Nonetheless, "the lack of publications in top-rates US journals is by no means a reflection of the 'quality' of the extant literature" (Kipping & Clark 2012). Over the past decade, sector restructuring has been significant and impressive. The movement into management and IT consulting markets by large non-consulting companies form the manufacturing, utilities and service sectors has turned into a trend. Additionally, the consulting industry has been shaped in recent years by the emergence and spectacular growth of the e-commerce and e-business consulting. (Kubr 2002)

4.2 Research Gaps and Issues

In accordance with the issue of a deficit of publications in North America, "consulting has yet to find its 'grand' theory' and, [...] is an industry difficult to put into databases - particularly due to its unclear and fluid boundaries, and partially due to the reluctance of the main actors to share information for fear of breaching client confidentiality" (Kipping & Clark 2012). Furthermore, "although there are underlying assumptions that culture plays an important role in management consulting, cultural aspects have not yet been addressed extensively in management consulting research" (Mohe 2008). Another aspect of consulting that presents an unexplored research field is knowledge creation potential. Knowledge management has become a key theme both in management literature as well as in corporate practice (Buono 2009). Regrettably, "only a small number of recent studies have shed light on the importance of the knowledge creation dynamics involved in the concrete implementation of management consulting interventions" (Buono 2009). Other mostly unexplored areas are ethics and gender as well as consulting in developing countries.

References

Abrahamson, E. (1991). Managerial fads and fashions: the diffusion and rejection of innovations. Academy of Management Review, 16/3.

Abrahamson, E. (1996). Management fashion. Academy of Management Review, 21/1.

Abrahamson, E. (2011). The iron cage: ugly, uncool, and unfashionable. Organization Studies, 32/5.

Armstrong, D. (2005). Organization in the mind: psychoanalysis, group relations, and organizational consultancy: occasional papers 1989 - 2003. Karmac Books.

Bader, J. (1996). Rethinking the consultant's role. In P.A. Comella, J. Bader, J.S. Ball, K. K. Wiseman, & R. R. Sagar (Eds.), The emotional side of organizations: Applications of Bowen family systems theory (pp. 18-24). Washington, DC: Georgetown Family Center.

Biech, E. (1999). The business of consulting. San Francisco: Jossey-Bass & Pfeiffer.

Biswas, S. & Twitchell, D. (2002). Management consulting: A complete guide to the industry (2nd ed.). New York: Wiley.

Buono, A. F. (2009). Emerging trends and issues in management consulting: consulting as a janus-faced reality. IAP. Available at: http://books.google.de/books?id=4X5fUvlGIIEC&dq=literature+consulting&source=gbs_n avlinks_s. (Accessed on: 01 March 2014).

Cummings, T. G. & Worley, C. G. (2009). Organization development and change. Cengage Learning. eBook. Available at: http://books.google.de/books?id=rdjtPTfkWG8C&dq=%22behavioral-science+knowledge+and+practices%22&source=gbs_navlinks_s. (Accessed 08 March 2014).

Day, J. D. (2004). Dynamics of the client-consultant relationship. In J.-P. Thommen & A. Richter (Eds.), Management consulting today - Strategies for a challenging environment (pp. 27 - 40). Wiesbaden: Gabler.

DiMaggio, P. J. & Powell, W. W. (1983). The iron cage revisited: Institutional isomorphism and collective rationality in organizations fields. American Sociological Review, 48 (2), pp. 147-160.

Faust, M. (2000). Warum boomt die Managementberatung? - Und warum nicht zu alien Zeiten und überall. SOFI-Mitteilungen Nr. 28/2000: 59-90. Available at: www.canhack.com.

Gould, L. J., Stapley, L. F., & Stein, M. (Eds.) (2001). The Systems Psychodynamics of Organizations: Integrating the Group Relations Approach, Psychoanalytic, and Open Systems Perspectives. London: Karnac.

Graubner, M. (2007). Task, firm size, and organizational structure in management consulting. European Business School Schloss Reichartshausen, Vol. 63. Springer eBook

Higdon, H. (1969). The Business Healers. New York: Random House.

Hofmann, M., von Rosenstiel, L. & Zapotoczky, K. (Eds.). (1991). Die sozio-kulturellen Rahmenbedingungen fuer Unternehmensberater. Stuttgart: Kohlhammer.

Kipping, M. & Clark, T. (2012). The Oxford handbook of management consulting. Oxford University Press. Available at: http://books.google.de/books?id=qGEz5tI_UygC&dq=origins+of+consulting&source=gbs_navlinks_s. (Accessed 15 March 2014).

Kipping, M. & Engwall, L. (2002). Management consulting : emergence and dynamics of a knowledge industry. Oxford University Press. Google eBook. Available at: http://books.google.de/books?id=ba_LE10UhagC&dq=relevant+literature+about+consulting&source=gbs_navlinks_s. (Accessed: 08 March 2014).

Kipping, M. & Armbruester, T. (1999). The consultancy field in Western Europe (No. 6 CEMP Report). Reading (U.K.): The University of Reading.

Kubr, M., (Ed.). (2002). Management consulting: A guide to the profession (4th ed.). Geneva: International Labour Office.

Lippitt, L. & Lippitt, R. (1978). The consulting process in action. University Associates.

Lowman, R. L. (17 Feb 2003). The California School of Organizational Studies handbook of organizational consulting psychology: a comprehensive guide to theory, skills, and techniques. John Wiley & Sons. Google eBook. Available at: http://books.google.de/books?id=vSQbaowow20C&dq=%22organizational+consulting%22&lr=&source=gbs_navlinks_s. (Accessed on: 01 March 2014).

McKenna, C. The origins of modern management consulting. The Johns Hopkins University. Available at: https://h-net.org/~business/bhcweb/publications/BEHprint/v024n1/p0051-p0058.pdf. (Accessed 16 March 2014).

Miller, J. (2008). J.A. The anxious organization: Why smart companies do dumb things (2nd ed.). Lanham, MD: Facts on Demand Press.

Mohe, M. (2008) Bridging the Cultural gap in management consulting research. International Journal of Cross Cultural Management vol. 8 no. 1 41-57.

Nevis, E. C. (2013). Organizational consulting: a gestalt approach. Taylor & Francis.

O'Shea, J. & Madigan, C. (1997). Dangerous company: The consulting powerhouses and the businesses they save and ruin. New York: Harper Business.

Ovans, A. (2011). Vision statement: the charts that changed the world. Harvard Business Review.

Peters, T. J. and Waterman Jr, R. H. (1982). In search of excellence: Lessons from american best-run companies. New York: Harper & Row.

Rasiel, E. M. (2001). The McKinsey way: using the techniques of the world's top strategy consultants to help you and your business. New York: McGraw Hill Professional.

Rowlinson, M. & Hassard, J. (2001). Marxist political economy, revolutionary politics, and labor process theory. Int. Studies of Mgt. & Org., vol. 30, no. 4, Winter 2000 - 2001, pp. 85 - 111. Available at: http://www.jstor.org/discover/10.2307/23316303?uid=3737864&uid=2&uid=4&sid=21103769251957. (Accessed on 28 March 2014).

Schein, E. H. (1987). Process consultation: Lessons for managers and consultants (Vol. 2). Reading (MA): Addison-Wesley.

Shodhganga.inflibnet.ac.in. Review of related literature. Available at: http://shodhganga.inflibnet.ac.in/bitstream/10603/3343/8/08_chapter%202.pdf. (Accessed on: 28 March 2014).

Szczerba, M. (2013). For key consulting concepts. The Gateway online. Available at: http://thegatewayonline.com/consulting/introducing-consulting/four-key-consulting-concepts. (Accessed on: 16 March 2014).

Tatum, M., (2014). What is organizational consulting?. wisegeek.com. Available at: http://www.wisegeek.com/what-is-organizational-consulting.htm#. (Accessed, 16 March 2014).

von Keller, E. & Lorentz, J. (1999). Zukunftsszenarien und Trends in der Mana- gementberatung. In G, Miiller-Stevens, J. Drolshammer & J. Kriegmeier (Eds.), Professional Service Firms: Wie sich multinationale Dienstleister positionieren (pp. 349-372). Frankfurt am Main: Frankfurter Allgemeine Zeitung Verlag.

Winum, P. C. & Nielsen, T. M. & Bradford, R. E.. Impact of organizational consulting. RHR International. Available at: http://www.c-suitefuture.com/sites/default/files/ImpactofOrganizationalConsulting(WinumNielsenBradford-HoOCP02').pdf. (Accessed on: 08 March 2014).

Wohlgemuth, A. C. (1995). Professionelle Unternehmensberatung: Eine zukunftsorientierte Dienstleistung. In A. C. Wohlgemuth & C. Treichler (Eds.), Unternehmensberatung und Management: Die Partnerschaft zum Erfolg (pp. 11-38). Zurich: Versus.

Ziegler, A. (1995). Beratung beim Wort genommen: Vom Sinn der Beratung. In A. C. Wohlgemuth & C. Treichler (Eds.), Unternehmensberatung und Management: Die Partnerschaft zum Erfolg (pp. 55-65). Zurich: Versus.

Change Agents

Xenia Davidoff, Patrick Bertram

Abstract. The interest in the process of planned change has created the professional role of the "change agent". This article attempts to reflect on the current state of this subject and to present both similar and contrasting views of researchers. While setting the context of a continuous change process model, the types and tasks of change agents are laid out. However, the emphasis will be on the effectiveness of change agents with a special focus on change resistance and managerial characteristics. In doing so, material was scanned spanning over 50 years of scholarly inquire. Some underexplored areas are highlighted and suggestions for future research made.

Keywords: Change agent, change consultant, change effectiveness, change implementation, change characteristics, change resistance

1 Introduction and Methodology

The Greek philosopher Heraclitus said, "There is nothing permanent except change" (Westover 2010, p. 45). It is obvious that the organizational environment will never again be stable and predictable (Gilley 2001). Organizations are continuously confronted with change as they have to stay competitive in a globalized economy. Figure depicts how the change process works by also emphasizing that change is of a continuous nature (McKenna 1994; Moorhead & Griffin 1992).

This interest in the process of planned change has also created a new professional role of the "change agent" (Westover 2010). Simply speaking, the change agent (CA) is a person "responsible for managing the change effort" (Moorhead & Griffin 1992, p. 501) by intersecting the organization and its business units irrespective of traditional hierarchies (Arrata, Despierre, & Kumra 2007). Referring to Figure 1, the CA is involved by the organization from the very beginning of the change process: Such a person continuously recognizes and defines the problem (in cooperation with the management), directly or indirectly implements new processes, entitles and trains employees, reaches out for resources necessary for the change effort and measures, evaluates and controls to what degree the change achieved the desired effect (Havelock & Zlotolow 1995; Jones 1969; McKenna 1994; Moorhead &

Griffin 1992). One of the change agent's major challenges is to overcome change resistance of organizational members, as will be discussed later.

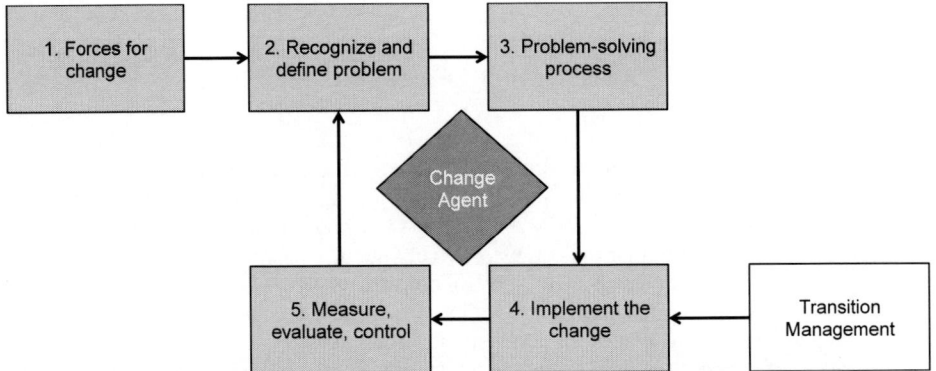

Figure 1: The continuous change process model (McKenna 1994; Moorhead & Griffin 1992)

There exist diverse views culminating in various types of change agents. One possible view is to distinguish between members of the organization (internal CAs), external consultants (Bennis 1966; Scurrah, Shani, & Zipfel 1971; Case, Vandenberg, & Meredith 2007; Holland 2000), or someone from the headquartes whom employees consider to be external (McKenna 1994). Meanwhile, Tichy (1975; 1976) proposed four different types of change agents relating to differences in diagnosing organizations:

1) Outside-pressure-type,

2) People-change-technology-type,

3) Analysis-for-the-top-type, and

4) Organization-development-type.

Other authors identified yet alternative typologies of change agents such as active propagators/passive propagators (Dupoux-Couturier, Quasnik, Redelsperger, & Vulpian 2011; Jones 1969) or homophilous/ heterophilous change agents (Duncan 1974). While much effort has been spent on identifying different types of change agents, more research is necessary regarding the effectiveness of those typologies.

After providing a definition, a task overview and different types for change agents, the question arises how change consultants actually manage change effectively. A popular format for providing information on the subject seems to be "the guide" – a list of elaborated characteristics of CAs, traits and techniques these consultants have to possess in order to overcome resistance and ensure effective organizational change. Therefore, this article closely examines the subject of "change agent theory" with prevailing literature addressing the nature of change resistancy of organisational members as the root source of why a CA is required followed by elaborated seven characteristics of change consultants in creating successful change effort. Research gaps are revealed throughout the article and are also summarized in the conclusion part, where also a critical evaluation on the topic will be provided (see figure 2).

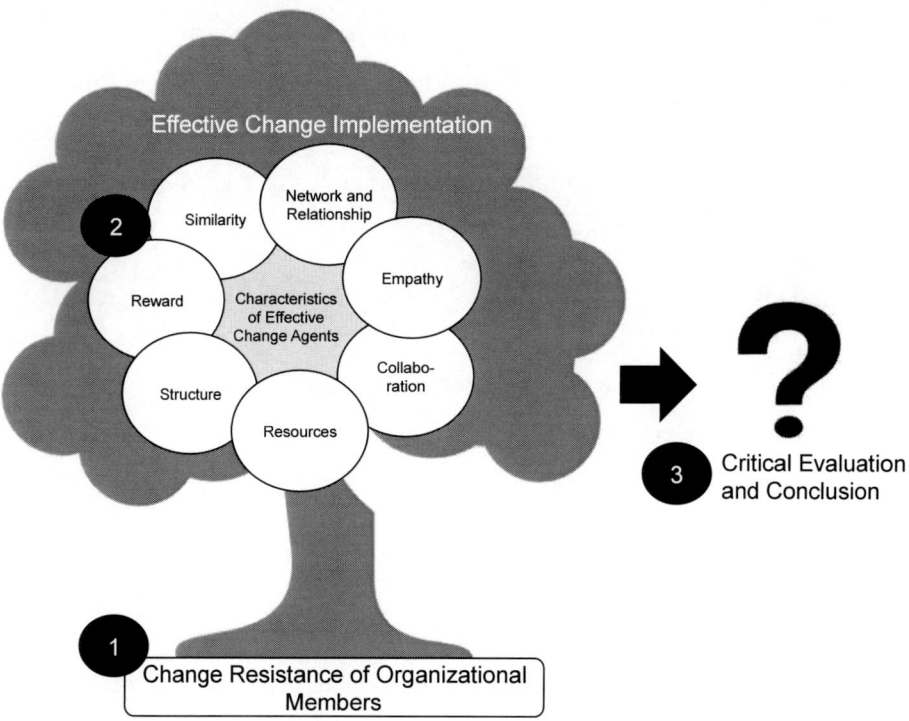

Figure 2: Structure of this article

2 Change Resistance as a Major Challenge of the Change Agent

Understanding people's resistance to change is fundamental in order to understand the agent's work in the organization. Change can frighten most people and this fear often "produces disruptions in organizations when the change is anticipated or announced" (Westover 2010, p. 50). Authors dealing with the "change agent" concept, often refer to the nature of change resistance as the root source of change agency work and provide guidance on how to overcome it (Ellis 2007; Stanleigh 2013; Schuler 2003).

Schuler (2003) proposed a list of reasons why people are resistant to change of which many are also found in other literature sources. Fore example, that change is seen as more risky than staying in the same direction; people fear that they do not have the competence to change and will fail; employees are overwhelmed and a proposed change can distract them from their work; people fear that change might have an impact on their quality of life, job status and security (Schuler 2003; Umble & Umble 2014). In order to manage this resistance, change agents need power and influence over the members of the organization (Ven & Poole 1995) in addition to special management characteristics which will be dealt with later on in this article.

With regard to change resistance, the success of internal change agents, in contrast to external change consultants, is discussed controversially among scholars. Internal change agents are mostly seen as effective in overcoming the resistance of change because of their better understanding of the operating procedures and of the company's history and employees (Bennis 1966; Holland 2000; Moorhead & Griffin 1992). Furthermore, advocates of the internal change agent argue that outside consultants are met by members of the organization with mistrust and suspicion. This implies that decisions made by internal change agents tend to be more accepted (Case, Vandenberg, & Meredith 2007). On the other hand, some authors are providing arguments in favor of outside consultants: they are not subdued to the company's politics, traditions and culture (Holland 2000); only skilled external consultants can provide the perspective and energy to implement change (Bennis

1966); they encourage to redefine the situation and identify unknown or challenging problem areas (Seashore 1961). Furthermore, findings by Case et al. (2007) have shown that "external change agents are more likely to utilize both human processual and techno- structural interventions " (Case et al. 2007, p. 14). In fact, the hypotheses by Scurrah et al. (1971) that outside change consultants would be associated with more conflict and would threaten the harmony has not truly been confirmed. Moorhead and Griffin (1992) even state that external agents are more popular among the employees because of their neutrality. Given the ongoing controversy, it would be desirable to engage in further investigations, which focus on the analysis of internal and external change agents in different change situations, industries and/or with different goals. Therefore, researchers could carry out numerous case studies of strategic changes existing in different organizations. Also, researchers could conduct questionnaire-based surveys at different stages of strategic change (Ford & Ford 2009).

3 Characteristics of Effective Change Agents

With a look at the availabl scholarly literature, on could say that several researchers have essentially diagnosed a set of seven characteristics that help overcome change resistance and effectively implement change. These factors concentrate on the way in which change consultants manage change and not on personal characteristics an agent may have. These characteristics are depicted in Figure 3. The suggested overlaps are to remind that these factors have to come together synergetically in order to create an effective outcome.

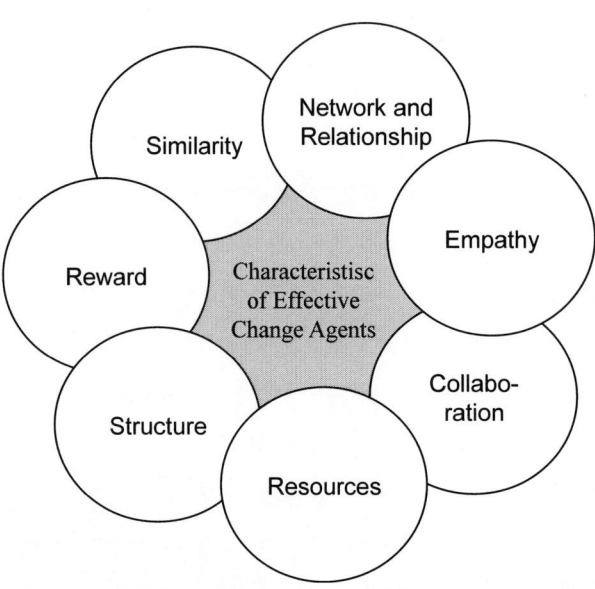

Figure 3: Characteristics of Effective Change Agents

3.1 Similarity

Havelock & Sashkin (1983) and Rogers (1983) identified that the more **similarities between the CA and the organizational members** exist, the higher the possibility that change will be successful. Rogers states that homophilic individuals, people who interact similar individuals, tend to communicate more effectively. However, controversy among authors regarding the effectiveness of homophily can be found. Granovetter (1973) identified hetereophily to be a strength. According to his findings, the strength of the 'weak ties' (group who does not share the same information and attributes) lies in carrying information among groups. Holland (2000) follows his findings and points out that during change, employees tend to find advice in the friendship network but evidence show that "in times of uncertainty, people prefer to seek information outside their immediate circle" (Holland 2000, p. 112).

3.2 Network and Relationship

The change agent's task domain includes both people and process. People are the key of organizational change and hence, a first critical step change agents have to make is the establishment of relationships with organizational members (Battilana & Casciaro 2010; 2012; 2013; Havelock & Zlotolow 1995; Rogers 1983; 1995; Rylatt 2013). Battilana & Casciaro (2010) see the benefit of emotional closeness not only as informational but also as political, since effective networking can help to influence potential endorsers and resisters of change. They diagnosed that CAs were much more effective when they had a good connection to these groups (Battilana et al. 2010). In contrast, Rogers (1983; 1995) places great emphasis on the relationship with opinion leaders. He defines them as individuals "who are able to influence other individuals' attitudes or overt behavior informally in a desired way with relative frequency" (Rogers 1995, p. 27). Identifying and mobilizing them leads more likely to success of the change consultant as opinion leaders have a significant effect on the mindset of their peers, which helps to promote change among employees (Rogers 1983; 1995; Lam and Schaubroeck 2000). However, Lam and Schaubroeck also mention that opinion leaders can be major obstacles as well.

Battilana & Casciaro (2012) propose that their findings regarding network effectiveness can be extended into various directions. For example, further investigations could benefit from larger samples; no self-selection of the change agent or complementary analysis with fully validated ego-network data or whole-network data. Furthermore, they diagnosed that a change agent has to establish a network in accordance with the change goal. Therefore, further investigations could examine to what extent the network has an impact on the change outcome in regards of different goals.

3.3 Empathy

As pointed out in the preceding sections, the success of change agents lies mainly not in technical expertise but in moving organizational members (Havelock & Zlotolow 1995; Moorhead & Griffin 1992). Researchers are generally aware that empathy, the skill of understanding the feelings of another person, plays a significant role in managing organizational change in. In his work, Rogers (1983) states that the success of the change agent is positively related to the empathy shown to organizational members. Engagement should not only be realized intellectually but also emotionally in order to achieve commitment of employees and to overcome change resistance (Smet et al. 2012). However, Rogers (1995) also mentions that showing empathy is hard to realize if the agent is too dissimilar from his clients, which is in line with the discussion presented in the section on "similarity" in this article.

3.4 Collaboration

Empathy also has the potential to tie the change agent with the employees in collaborative activities. Building participation and engagement through collaborative involvement is a highly emphasized characteristic of effective change agents in the literature. Several authors (Marrow et al. 1967; Kottler & Schlesinger 2008; Ford & Ford 2009; Anderson 2011; Foley 2013; Nastase et al. 2012) recommend that change agents should involve people in the change process by building participation and involvement through "leading steering committees, participating in staff education, engagement, and work redesign programs" (Rylatt 2013), as it leads to commitment, brings inspiration, innovation and empowerment. A study conducted by Rylatt (2013) shows that the higher performing change agents have a high amount of collaboration with their clients.

3.5 Resources

Resources in the form of time, energy and money are needed for successful change implementation but they are naturally limited (Havelock & Sashkin 1983; Rogers 1995). Some authors (Kottler & Schlesinger 2008; Zou & Lee 2008; Stanleigh 2013) mention and analyze cost and time aspects of change in their research. But only little empirical investigation has been carried out on what impact change agents characteristics (e.g. network / empathy) have on time, energy and costs of change implementation. As mentioned previously, Rogers (1983; 1995) observed that change agents tend to be more successful when they have a good relationship with opinion leaders. Here the question arises to what extent successful change implementation is linked to the resources of the change agent and of the organization.

Lam and Schaubroeck (2000) propose that a good relationship with opinion leaders can save costs of training employees considerably, because of their greater social access. Also efficient networking and effective collaboration activities can increase cost, time and energy efficiency, and thereby boost the change effort. In order to provide empirical more empirical evidence, researchers could examine the impact of a good relationship with opinion leaders (or other network groups) on training costs.

3.6 Structure

Besides the five previous factors, it is also necessary that change agents and organization members precisely plan and coordinate their activities in order to achieve efficient change implementation (Kottler & Schlesinger 2008; Maher & Hall 1998; Stanleigh 2013; Westover 2010). Change agents have to clearly define the need for change, as well as the required effort. Then the change quest becomes more likely to be understood and implemented by the organization (Stanleigh 2013). The competence of efficiently managing projects revealed a significant positive relationship with overall change performance. Effective communication can be achieved through advertising the needs and benefits of change more effectively (personally, and in written form), by educating employees beforehand and by engaging them into the planning process (Kottler & Schlesinger 2008; Stanleigh 2013). This is clearly connected with the "collaboration" factor earlier discussed. Referring back to the "capacity" factor, a good coordination structure of change activities can also save time, energy and money.

3.7 Reward and Change Incentives

Finally, change attempts can be constructed so that organizational members are rewarded for changing. Performance appraisals and non-financial reward systems belong to the human resource tools in aid of an effective change agent (Westover 2010). In contrast to non-financial rewards, Kottler & Schlesinger (2008) encourage to offer stimuli in form of higher wage rates in order to deal with resistance and to alter people's mindset about change. However, providing rewards and incentives for change in general is questionable as this might lead to some change in behavior but not to a change in the attitude (Nilakant & Ramnarayan 2006). Nonetheless, Nilakant and Ramnayaran suggest from their findings to provide incentives rather than discentives or punishment for change.

4 Critical Review and Conclusion

As the interest of planned change has grown in the last decades, so has the interest in change agents. Various topical streams have been studied about the effectiveness of change consultants. This article closely examined the topic of "change agents" with special focus on the effectiveness by examining factors relevant to change resistance, as well as characteristics of effective change agents, which have a positive impact on change efforts.

It was highlighted that the change resistance of organizational members can be seen as a major driver of the change agent's work. People have the tendcy to resist to change and certain management characteristics can help to overcome this resistance. Research has focused on both internal change agents and external consultants. Furthermore, there are also other categorizations of change agents requiring more empirical investigation.

In order to overcome change resistance and to implement change, seven characteristics of effective change agentry have been investigated with different authors offering differing perspectives. Nonetheless, it became clear that these characteristics are interdependent and have to be used synergetically in order to create an effective outcome. It is necessary to carry out more empirical work, since many authors provide guidance on techniques, traits and characteristics of CAs but only little empirical substance dealing with the impact of the interdependency of the elaborated characteristics on change effectiveness. This is why many questions arise: What effect does empathy have on the relationship and network of the change agent? What impact does the network of the change agent have on his or her resources? How do resources influence the outcome of the change effort? Are increased resource endowments enough to implement change successfully? The following model (see

Figure 4) summarizes revealed gaps, which help researchers to conduct further investigations.

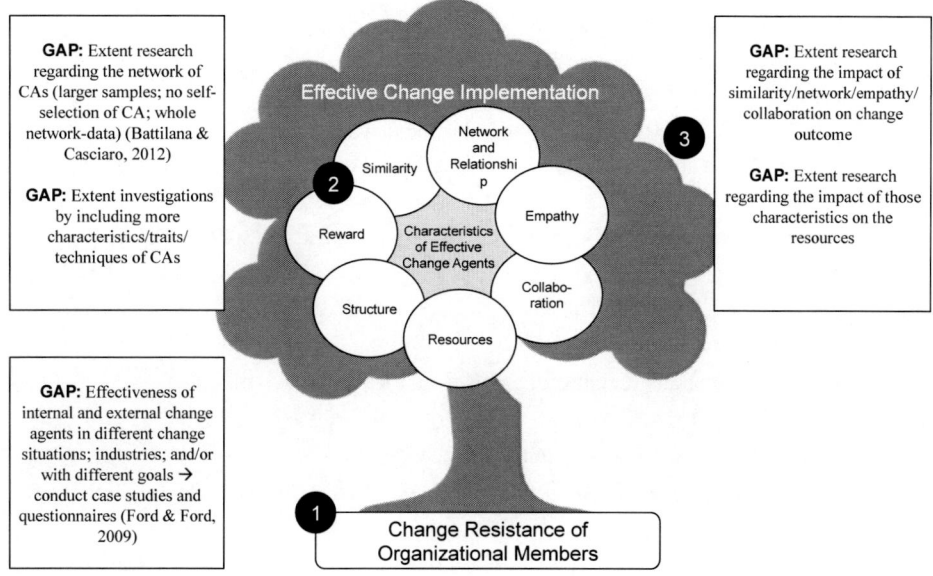

Figure 4: Research Gaps

References

Anderson, L. (2011). The Change Leader's Roadmap: How to Navigate Your Organization's Transformation. New York: Routledge.

Arrata, P., Despierre, A., & Kumra, G. (2007). Building an Effective Change Agent Team. McKinsey Quarterly, 39-43.

Battilana, J., & Casciaro, T. (2010). Power, Social Influence and Organizational Change: The Role of Network Position in Change Implementation. Academy of Management Annual Meeting Proceedings, 1-8.

Battilana, J. and Casciaro, T. (2012). Change agents, networks, and institutions: A Contingency Theory of Organizational Change. Academy of Management Journal, 55 (2), 381--398.

Battilana, J., & Casciaro, T. (2013). The Network Secrets of Great Change Agents. Harvard Business Review, 62-68.

Bennis, W. G. (1966). Changing Organizations. New York : McGraw-Hill.

Case, T. L., Vandenberg, R. J., & Meredith, P. H. (2007). Internal and External Change Agents. Leadership & Organization Development Journal, 4-15.

De Smet, A., Lavoie, J., & Hioe, E. S. (2012). Developing Better Change Leaders. McKinsey Quarterly (2), 98-104.

Duncan, R. B. (1974). Dimensions to Consider in Structuring the Change Agent's Role. Academy of Management Proceedings (1), pp. 50--50.

Dupoux-Couturier, Quasnik, Redelsperger, & Vulpian, d. (2011). A Particular Type of Change Agent. Reflections, 11 (1/2), 25-33.

Ellis, A. (2007). Overcoming Resistance. New York: Springer Pub.

Foley, N. (2013). Change Agent. Look for Four Telltale Traits. Leadership Excellence, 9.

Ford, J. D., & Ford, L. W. (2009). Decoding Resistance to Change. Harvard Business Review, 87 (4), 99-103.

Gilley, J. W. (2001). The Manager as Change Agent: A Practical Guide to Developing High-Performance People and Organizations. Cambridge: Perseus Publishing.

Grannovetter, M. (1973). The Strength of Weak Ties. American Journal of Sociology, 78 (6), 1360-1380.

Havelock, R. G., & Zlotolow, S. (1995). The Change Agent's Guide. New Jersey: Educational Technology Publications.

Holland, M. (2000). The Change Agent. In B. J. Reid, & W. Foster, Achieving Cultural Change in Networked Libraries (S. 105-107). Aldershot: Gower Publishing.

Jones, G. (1969). Planned Organizational Change: A Study in Change Dynamics. New York: Praeger.

Kottler, J. P., & Schlesinger, L. A. (2008). Choosing Strategies for Change. Harvard Business Review, 86 (7/8), 130-139.

Lam, S. S., & Schaubroeck, J. (2000). A Field Experiment Testing Frontline Opinion Leaders as Change Agents. Journal of Applied Psychology, 85 (6), 987-995.

Havelock & Sahskin (1983) in Lunenburg, F. C. and Irby, B. J. (2006). The Principalship: Vision to Action. Belmont, CA: Thomson/Wadsworth.

Maher, H., & Hall, P. (1998). Agents of Change. Dublin: Oak Tree Press.

Marrow, A. J., Bowers, D. G., & Seashore, S. E. (1967). Management by Participation: Creating a Climate for Personal and Organizational Development. New York: Harper & Row.

McKenna, E. (1994). Business Psychology and Organisational Behaviour. Hove, UK: Lawrence Erlbaum.

Moorhead, G., & Griffin, R. W. (1992). Organizational Behavior. Boston: Houghton Mifflin.

Nastase, M., Guiclea, M., & Bold, O. (2012). The Impact of Change Management in Organizations - a Survey of Methods and Techniques for a Successful Change. Review of International Comparative Management / Revista de Management Comparat International, 13 (1), 5-16.

Nilakant, V., & Ramnarayan, S. (2006). Change Management. New Delhi: Response Books.

Rogers, E. (1995). Diffusion of innovations (4th edition). New York: The Free Press.

Rogers, E. M. (1983). Diffusion of Innovations (3rd edition). New York: Free Press.

Rylatt, A. (2013). Three Qualities of Highly Successful Change Agents. T+D , 67 (7), 72-74.

Schuler, A. (2003). Overcoming Resistance to Change: Top Ten Reasons for Change Resistance. Abgerufen am 25. 03 2014 von Schuler Solutions, Inc.: http://www.schulersolutions.com/resistance_to_change.html

Scurrah, M. J., Shani, M., & Zipfel, C. (1971). Influence of Internal and External Change Agents in a Simulated Educational Organization. Administrative Science Quarterly, 16 (1), 113-120.

Seashore, C., & Van Egmond, E. (1961). The Consultant-Trainer Role. In G. Bennis, K. Benne, & R. Chin, The Planning of Change (S. 660-666). New York: Holt Rinehart and Winston.

Stanleigh, M. (2013). Leading Change. Journal for Quality & Participation, 36 (2), 39-40.

Thomas, C. J. (2014). Cognitive, Affective, and Behavioral Responses to Organizational Change. Supervision, 75 (3), 3-7.

Tichy, N. M. (1975). How Different Types of Change Agents Diagnose Organizations. Human Relations, 28 (9), 771-799.

Tichy, N. M. (1976). Stand When Your Number is Called. Human Relations, 29 (10), 945-967.

Umble , M., & Umble, E. (2014). Overcoming Resistance to Change. Industrial Management, 56 (1), 16-21.

Ven, A. V., & Poole, M. (1995). Explaining Development and Change in Organizations. Academy of Management Review, 510-540.

Westover, J. H. (2010). Managing Organizational Change: Change Agent Strategies and Techniques to Successfully Managing the Dynamics of Stability and Change in Organizations. International Journal of Management and Innovation, 2 (1), 45-50.

Zou, Y., & Lee, S.-H. (2008). The Impacts of Change Management Practices on Project Change Cost Performance. Construction Management & Economics, 26 (4), 387-393.

Organizational Learning

Daniel Dierkes, Christian Enderle

Abstract. Due to fast-paced, changing, competitive and unpredictable business environments, organizations need to be highly adaptable and must continue to improve. Hence, the discipline of a learning organization (LO) and organizational learning (OL) increasingly stepped into the center of attention. After the first works on the topic of learning in the context of organizations in the 1960s, it became a prominent point of discussion from which the volume of publications on the concept of OL, as well as the acceptance and definitions of the concept were growing. However, the concept of OL is very broad comprising for almost all aspects of organizational change.

Keywords: Organizational learning, learning organization, corporation, change change management

1 Introduction

Due to fast-paced changing, competitive and unpredictable business environments, organizations need to be highly adaptable and continue to improve. Hence, the discipline of a learning organization (LO) and organizational learning (OL) increasingly stepped into the center of attention. After Cangelosi and Dill (1965) first worked on the topic of learning in the context of organizations, it became a prominent point of discussion from which the volume of publications on the concept of OL (Crossan & Guato 1996) as well as the acceptance and definitions of the concept were growing (Dodgson 1993). However, the concept of OL is very broad comprising for almost all aspects of organizational change (Wang & Ahmed 2002). In fact, the general conceptual framework emerged from contributions from both scientists and practitioners (Spector & Davidsen 2005).

2 Classification of Organizational Learning and Related Terms

According to Spector and Davidsen (2005), the foundations of OL are shaped by various disciplines such as: observable behavior and higher order functions (Cyert & March 1963), decision making and ambiguity (March & Olsen 1975), feedback and reflective mechanisms (Agyris & Schoen 1975), cultural, environmental and sociological contexts of change (March & Levitt 1995), organic and dynamic aspects of organizations (Senge 1990), as well as different models of a learning organization (Morecroft & Sterman 1994). In the following, a closer look at the notions of individual learning, knowledge management, and the learning organization will be provided.

2.1 Individual Learning

According to Spector and Davidsen (2005), the individual learning process acts as a kind of prerequisite for OL, which can be defined as an "ongoing process of forming, storing, retrieving and modifying mental models and schemas in response to the dynamics of the situation and environment (Spector & Davidsen 2005. P. 66)." Hence, in order to facilitate OL, one need to consider the individual learning process. However, individual learning does not necessarily foster OL (Ikehara 1999) as wrong learning might also negatively impact an organization (Field 1997). Therefore, the LO itself needs to incorporate individual learning into OL (Wang & Ahmed 2002).

2.2 Knowledge Management

Knowledge management and OL are two parallel developed concepts which often refer to each other (Wang & Ahmed 2003) and even though knowledge management does not naturally belong to the field of OL, it is very closely connected and a critical aspect on how organizational learning functions (Gilson et al. 2009). Knowledge management is the process by which knowledge is first recognized, categorized and captured (Gilson et al. 2009) whereby a majority of the knowledge will be stored in the minds of individual members of the organizations (Nonaka & Takeuchi 1996).

2.3 Learning Organization

Sun (2003) noticed that a lot of companies do not differentiate between the terms learning organization and organizational learning. Hence, (Valaski et al. 2012) state that both concepts are often considered being complementary among scholars (Finger & Buergin 1998; Latheemaki et al. 2001). The concept of a LO arose in the

1990's and was influenced by scholars such as (Pedler et al. 1991) and Senge (1990).

Sun (2003) linguistically defines OL as a learning process of an organization by which the organization learns in a collective (organizational) way, whereas the term LO basically stands for an organization that is currently learning or in the process of learning. Some scholars argue that, the term of a LO is an ideal concept, which organizations shall achieve in order to reach a continuous learning state (Finger & Buergin, 1998), which is characterized by behavioral changes within the organization as a resulting effect of learning (Reynolds & Ablett 1998). Gorelick (2005) in this context argues that, Senge's five disciplines: personal mastery, mental models, shared vision, team learning and system thinking shall be central components in a learning organization (Senge 1990) providing applicable tools and methods for the process of organizational learning. Gorelick (2005) further notes that OL and LO should co-exist and that in order to be an effective LO, organizations need a deep learning cycle and further must recognize that to reach such state is a very time consuming task.

3 Conceptual Frameworks of Organizational Learning

Lloria and Moreno-Luzon (2013) underscore that contributions to the specifications of OL arose from various scholars and account for aspects such as the ontological levels, the modes of knowledge creation, the sub-processes of learning, the explicit and tacit dimension of knowledge, as well as the different types of learning.

3.1 Single-loop learning, Double-loop learning and Deutero-learning

The literature of OL has paid particular attention to the idea of learning loops (Gilson et al., 2009). Agyris & Schoen (1978) defined their perspective on OL with the three complementary levels of single-loop (adaptive) learning, double-loop (generative) learning and deuteron-learning (Agyris & Schoen 1978), illustrated in figure 1 below. Single-loop learning is the identification and correction of mistakes within existing structures of an organization (Maden 2012). These processes take place when firms first monitor how they are performing in detail to then reflect to identify areas of improvement (Gilson et al. 2009). In this context, (Greve 2003) states that organizations tend to look for problem solutions from their immediate neighborhood, or they look for previously originated problems to then apply exact solutions to the current problem. (Gilson et al. 2009, P.17) call the phenomena "the garbage can approach to organizational learning", stating that within organizations there may already exist advocates for particular problem solutions. On a next level, double-loop learning goes beyond the general process monitoring, questions more widely organizational problems and seeks to find permanent solutions to sources of error or under-performance (Gilson et al. 2009). Thus, the double-loop process facilitates openness, flexibility and autonomy within an organization (Beeby & Booth, 2000). For some scholars such as (Nonaka & Takeuchi 1995) the distinction between single and double-loop learning is vague because in practice the staff of an organization is often not encouraged to ask broader range questions (Gilson et al. 2009). Deutero-learning or as (Gilson et al. 2009) name it triple-loop (strategic) learning is the final stage of the learning loop approach. This level involves the reflection of previous experiences on OL (Maden 2012), questioning their underlying assumptions, principles and organizational beliefs (Gilson et al. 2009).

Many models of OL focus on single and double-loop learning, with almost no focus on higher (triple-loop) levels of learning (Kenny 2006). Hence, continuous improvement within organizations will further take place, however, in order to move ahead competitors, an organization's strategy should also focus on innovation and thus take triple-loop learning into account (Wang & Ahmed 2003).

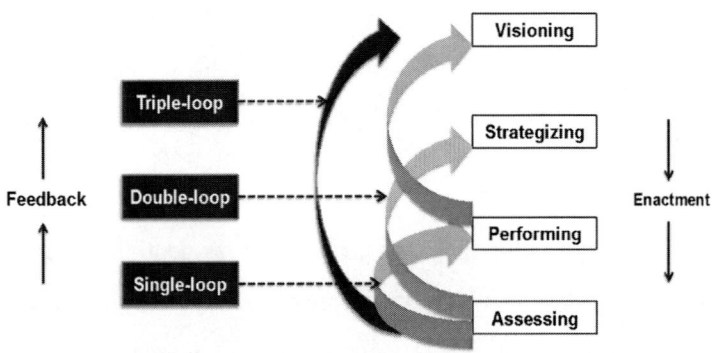

Figure 1: The idea of learning loops, adapted from Source: (Agyris & Schoen 1978; Torbert 1999), own illustration.

3.2 The Ontological Levels of Learning

The ontological levels of learning comprise an individual, group, organizational and inter-organizational level (Nonaka 1994), whereas the individual, group and organizational level interact with each other and thus constitute the feed-forward process from the individual to the organizational level and in the same way the downward process from the organizational to the individual level, which defines the feedback process (Crossan et al. 1999; Bontis et al. 2002). Thus, the constant ebb and flow of the feed-forward and downward processes gives OL the feature of a dynamic process (Lloria & Moreno-Luzon 2013).

3.3 The Modes of Knowledge Conversion

The modes of knowledge conversion are socialization, externalization, combination and internationalization (Nonaka 1994). Nonaka (1994) further assumes that at an epistemological dimension, knowledge emerges through the conversion between tacit and explicit knowledge, whereas the knowledge creation process is a dynamic process comprising four modes of knowledge conversion: 1) Socialization, from tacit knowledge to tacit knowledge; 2) Combination, from explicit knowledge to explicit knowledge; 3) Externalization from tacit knowledge to explicit knowledge;

and 4) Internalization, from explicit knowledge to tacit knowledge (Nonaka 1994 P.18). Thus knowledge creation within an organization originates with the tacit knowledge of individuals, organizations than need to mobilize the knowledge to the group, organizational and inter-organizational (ontological) levels, which (Nonaka & Takeuchi 1995 P. 73) call the "spiral of organizational knowledge creation".

3.4 The Learning Sub-Processes

The ontological dimension is also the base for another influential OL model from Crossan et al. (1999), which later was part of the research from many other authors such as Bontis et al. (2002) and Choo & Bontis (2002). The most relevant characteristic of the model is the identification of the four learning processes: intuiting, interpreting, integrating and institutionalizing. The so-called 4I framework of OL suggested by Crossan et al. (1999) possess the following four components: 1) Intuiting, which stands for a characteristic of learning at an individual level whereas a recognition of a pattern or from personal experience is required; 2) Interpreting which serves as a bridge between the individual and the group level through explaining the idea with words or actions; 3) Integrating stands as a meeting point for the group and organizational level at which a shared understanding is developed and 4) Institutionalizing takes place at the organizational level at which routines are developed which further ideally serve as guidelines for the organization (Lloria & Moreno-Luzon 2013).

3.5 The Learning Typologies

Another relevant distinction has to be made between OL typologies, which were first introduced by March (1991) who differentiates between exploitation and exploration. The learning transfers among the above mentioned 4I framework processes are closely related to exploration and exploitation. Exploitation thereby stands for learning through a specific search, an improvement of something already existing or the transfer of already institutionalized OL, whereas the concept of exploration means to learn completely new processes through experimentation and interpretation (March 1991; Lewin et al. 1999; Crossan & Bedrow 2003). In this context, various authors highlight the tension between exploration and exploitation as they compete for different organizational resources (Gibson & Birkinshaw 2004).

3.6 The Information Processing Perspective (System View)

Another perspective that underlies many studies is the OL process defined by Huber (1991). He as well as Cyert & March (1963), have a system view on OL and see OL mainly from an information processing perspective (Jerez-Gomez et al. 2005). Huber (1991) defines the four components of the OL process as: knowledge acquisition, information distribution, information interpretation and organizational memory – whereby the components knowledge acquisition, information distribution and information interpretation are all dependent on organizational memory. Huber further states that OL is an intentional process and thus learning not always increases the potential effectiveness, given the fact that learning may take place incorrectly. Another idea stressed by Friedlander (1983: 194) is that learning may not lead to "observable changes in behavior" meaning that learning may result in new and significant insights and awareness that dictate no behavioral change". Within the system view the sub-streams of an open system and closed systems are identified. Within the closed system OL solely takes place within an organization, whereas the open system's view point reflects the contingency approach to organizational learning in which knowledge is acquired from both the outside and the inside of an organization (Wang & Ahmed 2003).

4 Measuring Organizational Learning

One of the traditional ways of measuring learning has been the so-called learning curves (Lieberman 1987) and experiences curves (The Boston Consulting Group 1973). However (Garvin 1993: 89) defines the curves as "incomplete measuring tools" because they solely concentrate on learning by doing and only measure the results obtained. Learning also has been measured by taking other variables such as the number of patents (Decarolis & Deeds 1999) or the R&D expenditure (Bierly & Chakrabati1996) into account. All techniques rather focus on process outcomes than on the actual learning process even though the learning process is multidimensional with multiple sub processes (Slater & Narver 1994). Jimenez & Sanz-Valle (2011) point out that a variety of authors put a lot of emphasis on the key role of both innovation (Baker & Sinkula 2002) and OL (Dodgson, 1993; Garvin, 1993) for enhancing a company's competitive advantage and organizational performance. Going in the same direction, some studies argue that OL and its output, organizational knowledge, Jimenez Sanz-Valle (2011) are preliminary stages of innovation (Baker & Sinkula 2002; Nonaka & Takeuchi 1995). The literature not only proposes a positive relationship between OL and performance but suggests that innovation is mediating the relation between the two variables (Jimenez & Sanz-Valle 2011). Therefore, some authors propose that organizational learning allows companies to develop capabilities that prosper innovation and then innovation positively affects organizational performance (Baker & Sinkula 2002; Hurley & Hult 1998). The findings of Jimenez & Sanz-Valle only recently provide additional evidence to existing conclusions that show a positive relationship between both OL and performance (Bontis et al. 2002; Baker & Sinkula 1999; Keskin 2006) as well as between OL and innovation (Hurley & Hult 1998; Keskin 2006). However, Jimenez and Sanz-Valle point out that only little data is available which analyzes the relationships between those variables empirically. More, their findings show that OL has greater influence on innovation than on performance, suggesting that OL may influence organizational performance mainly by enhancing innovation (Jimenez & Sanz-Valle 2011).

5 Research Gaps

Even though there exist differences on emphasis among authors, "organizational learning itself is generally accepted as a good thing" (Gilson et al. 2009, P.7). One of the main disputes among authors are the different viewpoints on the enabling components for organizations to become a 'learning organization', as well as a lack of concurrence with regard to the components that define the concept and accurate measurements to quantify OL.

Moreover, many scholars underscore the need for research on several aspects, such as more empirical investigations on how OL can be encouraged and maximized, and how organizations may become true learning organizations (Pun & Nathai-Balkissoon 2011). Additionally, due to the fast pacing and ever changing nature of business environments a couple of authors call for a wider-ranging approach toward)08), comp 2). A sumr

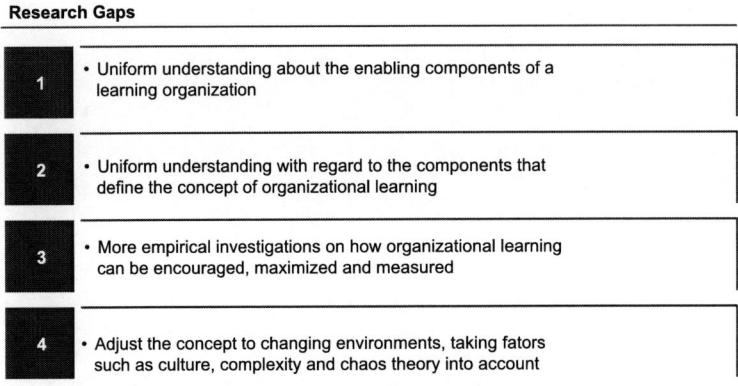

Figure 2: Summary of identified research gaps (Source: own illustration)

6 Summary and Conclusion

As mentioned within the analysis of research gaps, most studies lack conformance with the components that define the concept of OL. Thus the influential contributions dominate the design of the concept. From the analysis of such influential contributions, four key focus areas seem to cover the concept of OL:

1. Ontological levels of Learning, including feedback and feed-forward flows (Nonaka 1994; Crossan et al. 1999)
2. Modes of Knowledge Conversion (Nonaka 1994)
3. Learning Sub-Processes (Crossan et al. 1999)
4. Learning Typologies (March 1991)

Finally, because of the diverse origins of the field and the disagreements among scholars regarding the components of OL, it seems unlikely that a common uniform understanding will be shared widely in the near future.

References

Argyris, C., & Schoen, D. (1978). *Organisational learning: a theory of action perspective.* New York: Addison-Wesley.

Baker, W. E., & Sinkula, J. M. (2002). Market orientation, learning orientation and product innovation: delving into the organization's black box. *Journal of Market-Focussed Management , 5* (1), 5-23.

Baker, W. E., & Sinkula, J. M. (1999). The synergistic effect of market orientation and learning orientation on organizational performance. *Journal of the Academy of Marketing Science, 27* (4), 411-427.

Beeby, M., & Booth, C. (2000). Networks and interorganizational learning: A critical review. *The Learning Organization , 7* (2), 75-88.

Bierly, P., & Chakrabarti, A. (1996). Generic knowledge strategies in the US pharmaceutical industry. *Strategy Management Journal , 17*, 123-135.

Bontis, N., Crossan, M. M., & Hulland, J. (2002). Managing an organizational learning system by aligning stocks and flows. *Journals of Management Studies , 39* (4), 437-469.

Cyert, R., & March, J. (1963). *A behavioral theory of the firm* (2nd Edition ed.). Malden, MA, USA: Blackwell.

Cangelosi, V. E., & Dill, W. R. (1965). Organizational Learning: Obersavtions toward a theory. *Administrative Science Quarterly , 10* (2), 175-203.

Choo, C. W., & Bontis, N. (2002). *The strategic management of intellectual capital and organizational knowledge.* Oxford: Oxford University Press.

Cohen, M., & Sproul, L. (1991). Editors introduction. *Organization Science - Special Issue on Organisational Learning , 2* (1), 1-3.

Crossan, M. M., Lane, H. W., & White, R. (1999). Organizational learning framework: from intuition to institution. *Academy of Management Review , 3* (24), 522-537.

Crossan, M., & Berdrow, I. (2003). Organizational learning and strategic renewal. *Strategic Management Journal , 24* (1), 1087-1105.

Crossan, M., & Guatto, T. (1996). Organizational Learning Profile. *Journal of Organizational Change Management , 9* (1), 107-122.

Decarolis, D. M., & Deeds, D. L. (1999). The impact of stocks and flows of organizational knowledge on firm performance: an empirical investigation of the bio-technology industry. *Strategy Management Journal , 20*, 953-968.

Dodgson, M. (1993). Organizational Learning: A Review of Some Literatures. *Organization Studies , 14* (3), 375-394.

Field, L. (1997). Impediments to empowerment and learning within organisations. *The Learning Organisation , 4* (4), 149-158.

Finger, M., & Buergin, S. (1998). *The concept of the "Leaning Organization" applied to the transformation of the public sector: Conceptual contributions for theory development. .* London: Sage.

Fitzgerald, L., & Van Eijnatten, F. M. (2002). Chaos speak: a glossary of chaordic terms and phrases. *Journal of Organizational Change Management , 15* (4), 412-423.

Friedlander, F. (1983). *Patterns of Individual and Organizational Learning.* San Francisco: Jossey-Bass.

Garvin, D. (1993, July/August). Building a learning organization. *Harvard Business Review*, 78-91.

Gibson, C. B., & Birkinshaw, J. (2004). The antecedents consequences, and mediating role of organizational ambidexterity. *Academy of Management Journal, 47* (1), 209-226.

Gilson, C., Dunleavy, P., & Tinkler, J. (2009). *Organizational Learning in Goverment Sector Organizations: Literature Review.* London School of Economics Public Policy Group. London: LSE Public Policy Group.

Gorelick, C. (2005). Organizational learning vs the learning organization: a conversation with a practionier. *The Learning Organization, 12* (4), 383-388.

Greve, H. R. (2003). *Organizational Learning from Performance Feedback: A Behavioural Perspective on Innovation and Change.* Cambridge: Cambridge University Press.

Ikehara, H. (1999). Implications of Gestalt theory and practice for the learning organisation. *The Learning Organisation, 2* (6), 63-69.

Huber, G. (1991). Organizational Learning: The Contributing Processes and the Literatures. *Organization Science, 1* (2), 88-115.

Hurley, R. E., & Hult, G. T. (1998). Innovation, market orientation and organizational learning: an integration and empirical examination. *Journal of Marketing, 62,* 42-54.

Jerez-Gomez, P., Lorente, J., & Valle-Cabrera, R. (2005). Organizational learning capability: a proposal of measurement. *Journal of Business Research* (58), 715-725.

Jimenez, D., & Sanz-Valle, R. (2011). Innovation, organizational learning and Performance. *journal of Business Research* (64).

Kenny, J. (2006). "Strategy and the learning organisation: a maturity model for the formation of strategy". *The Learning Organization, 13* (4), 353-368.

Keskin, H. (2006). Market orientation, learning orientation, and innovation capabilities in SMEs. *European Journal of Innovation Management, 9* (4), 396-417.

Latheemaki, S., Toivonen, J., & Mattila, M. (2001). Critical aspects of organizational learning research and proposals for its measurement. *British Journal of Management, 12* (2), 113-129.

Lewin, A. Y., Long, C. P., & Carroll, T. (1999). The co-evolution of new organizational forms. *Organization Science, 10* (1), 535-550.

Lieberman, M. (1987). The Learning Curve, Diffusion, And Competitive Strategy. *Strategic Management Journal, 8,* 441-452.

Lloria, B., & Moreno-Luzon, M. (2013). Organizational learning: Proposal of an integrative scale and research instrument. *Journal of Business Research* (67), 692-697.

Nonaka, I. (1994). A dynamic theory of organizational knowledge creation. *Organization Science, 5* (1), 14-37.

Nonaka, I., & Takeuchi, H. (1995). *The knowledge-creating company: How Japanese companies create the dynamics of innovation.* New York-Oxfrod: Oxford University Press.

Maden, C. (2012). Transforming Public Organizations into Learning Organizations: A Conceptual Model. *Public Organization Review* (12), 71-84.

March, J. G. (1991). Exploration and exploitation in organizational learning. *Organization Science*, *2* (1), 71-87.

March, J., & Levitt, B. (1988). Organisational learning. *Annual Review of Sociology*, *14*, 319-340.

March, J., & Olsen, J. (1975). The uncertainty of the past: Organizational learning under ambiguity. *European Journal of Political Research* (3), 147-171.

Morecroft, J. W., & Sterman, J. D. (1994). *Modeling for learning organizations.* Portland, USA: Productivity Press.

Pun, K. F., & Nathai-Balkissoon, M. (2011). Integrating knowledge management into organisational learning. *The Learning Organization*, *18* (3), 203-223.

Pedler, M., Burgoyne, J., & Boydell, T. (1991). *The Learning Company.* New York: McGraw-Hil.

Sun, H. C. (2003). Conceptual clarifications for organizational learning, learning organization and a learning organization. *Human Resource Development International*, *6* (2), 153-166.

Senge, P. (1990). *The fifth discipline. The art and practice of the learning organization.* New York, New York, USA: Doubleday.

Slater, S. F., & Narver, J. C. (1994). Market Oriented Isn't Enough: Build a Learning Organization. *Marketing Science Institute*, 94-103.

Spector, J., & Davidsen, P. (2005). *How can organizational learning be modeled and measured?* Florida State University ; University of Bergen. Amsterdam: Elsevier.

Reynolds, R., & Ablett, A. (1998). Transforming the rhetoric of organisational learning to the reality of the learning organisation. *The Learning Organization*, *5* (1), 24-35.

The Boston Consulting Group. (1973). *The Experience Curve- Reviewed.* (T. B. Group, Producer) Retrieved 3 20, 2014, from bcg perspectives: www.bcgperspectives.com/content/classics/corporate_finance_corporate_strategy_portfolio_management_the_experience_curve_reviewed_history/

Torbert, W. R. (1999). The distinctive questions developmental action inquiry asks. *Management Learning*, *30* (2), 189-206.

Valaski, J., Malucelli, S., & Reinehr, S. (2012). Ontologies application in organizational learning. A literature Review. *Expert Systems with Applications* (39), 7555-7561.

Walczak, S. (2008). Knowledge management and organizational learning. *The Learning Organization*, *15* (6), 486-494.

Wang, C. L., & Ahmed, P. K. (2003). Organisational learning: a critical review. *The Learning Organization*, *10* (1), 8-17.

Wang, C., & Ahmed, P. (2002). *A Review of the Concept of Organisational Learning.* Wolverhampton Business School, Management Research Centre. Wolverhampton: University of Wolverhampton.

Turnaround Management

Michaela Kegel, Lukas Söntgerath

Abstract. Managing crisis and declining situations has been relevant ever since people started to do business. This article seeks to provide an overview of existing literature on turnaround management. By definition, "turnaround management is the systematic and rapid implementation of a range of measures to correct a seriously unprofitable situation. It might include dealing with a financial disaster or measures to avoid the highly likely occurrence of such a disaster" (Arpi 1999). Within this field of study, researchers dedicated considerable effort to the root causes of decline and the influence on the turnaround process. Moreover, different management approaches and models will be discussed within the following contribution. Hereby two main research streams could be identified: proponents of consistent application of retrenchment strategies to overcome turnaround situations and supporters of adaptive strategies depending on the business environment.

Keywords: Turnaround management, crisis, turnaround, management, change, radical, problem

1 Introduction

Managing crisis and declining situations has been relevant ever since people started to do business. With continuously growing industries and highly competitive markets on a global scale, turnaround management has become more crucial than ever (Arpi 1999). This article seeks to provide an overview of existing literature on turnaround management. It starts with a brief definition of relevant terms followed by an examination of response strategies and actions. Finally, this article closes with a quick summary of the main research findings within the field of turnaround management.

2 Definition of Turnaround Management

The following definitions of turnaround management provide a comprehensive definition that is in line with and cited by recent literature.

"Turnaround management is the systematic and rapid implementation of a range of measures to correct a seriously unprofitable situation. It might include dealing with a financial disaster or measures to avoid the highly likely occurrence of such a disaster" (Arpi 1999). According to Pearce and Robbins (1993) turnaround management deals with the pursuit of recovery of an organizational decline, whereas the recovery from decline is defined as turnaround. In turn, "organizational decline is a condition in which a substantial, absolute decrease in an organization's resource base occurs over a specified period of time." (Cameron, Kim & Whetten 1987, in line with D' Aveni 1989). "Decrease in resources base" refers mainly to financial and managerial (human) resources (D'Aveni 1989).

Schendel (1976) was one of the first researchers known in the field of turnaround and published several early research papers in cooperation with other authors. According to his studies, a performance decline is described as a strategic decision problem that needs to be addressed with a turnaround strategy. This strategy has to be aligned with the corporate problems, which can be classified either as "strategic" or "operational" – often referred to as "external" and "internal" or "firm-based" and "industry-based" (Schendel et al. 1976, Schendel & Patton 1975/76, Hofer & Schendel, 1978, Hofer 1980, Cameron et al. 1988, Arogyaswamy, Barker & Yasai-Ardekani 1995). Decline phases may occur gradually over a long period of time or abruptly, e.g. due to an economic crisis. Research shows that particularly large organizations can easily be caught in a downward spiral of decline for a longer period of time (Hambrick & D'Aveni 1988).

3 Turnaround Strategies and Processes

In turnaround situations, where business performance is persistently "below some minimal acceptance level" (Hambrick 1985, p.22), appropriate strategy selection and its implementation is of great importance. Relevant turnaround strategies discussed in literature are highlighted in the following.

3.1 Turnaround Strategies

Existing proposals on turnaround strategies mainly involve two main strategy approaches: retrenchment (of costs/assets) and growth. Retrenchment triggered highly controversial discussions regarding the strategy's contribution to recovery, especially to increasing performance. Pearce and Robbins (1992) define retrenchment as a basic strategy that represents the first stage of their *two-stage turnaround model*. Within their framework, retrenchment of costs and/or assets is then addressed in a second stage followed by strategic actions (see Figure 1).

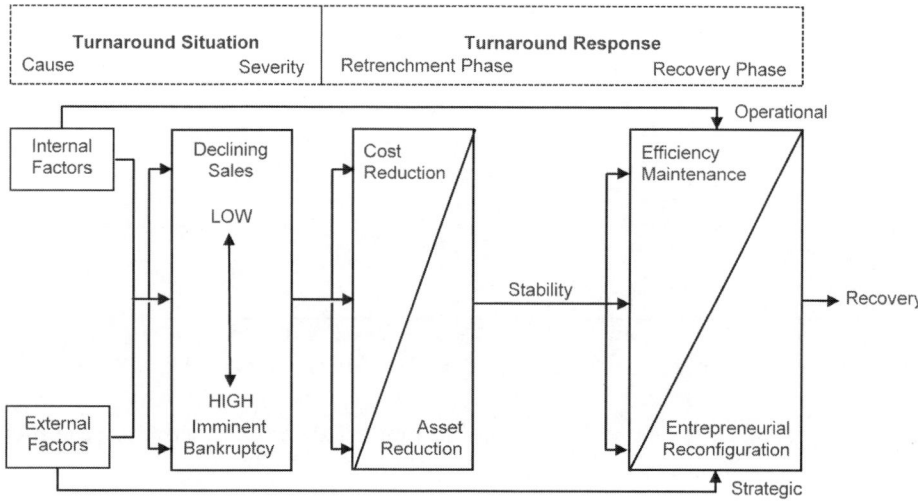

Figure 1: Turnaround situation and response adapted from Pearce and Robbins 1993

Although the model is cited in numerous research papers, it is also criticized as representing a limited view. Barker III. and Mone (1994), as well as Arogyaswamy et al. (1995), argue that retrenchment is not imperatively necessary in all turnaround processes but rather seen as a consequence of decreasing performance. A study revealed that non-turnaround organizations cut back their operations to an even higher extent than turnaround organizations and that, if poorly managed, cutbacks worsened a decline situation (Arogyaswamy & Yasai-Ardekani, 1997, Barker III. & Mone 1994). Figure 2 below shows a contingency model adapted from Arogyaswamy et al. (1995).

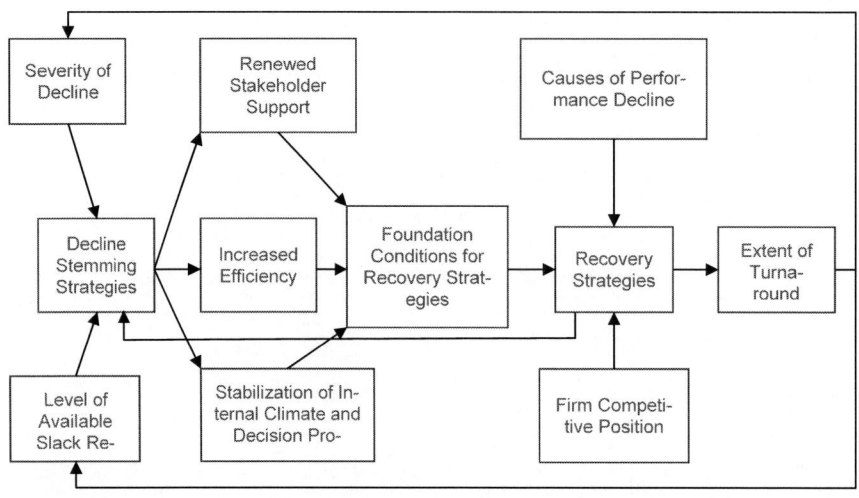

Figure 2: Two-stage Contingency Model (adapted from Arogyaswamy et al. 1995)

Khandwalla (1992) even came to the finding that organizations may increase their business activity in the turnaround process. Furthermore, Arogyaswamy et al. (1995) state that the process is not necessarily performed in an often suggested, sequential order. They put forward the idea of an interacting, interdependent model and identified two classes of response-strategies to manage a turnaround situation: decline-stemming strategies to reverse dysfunction, and recovery strategies to enhance the performance compared to competitors. The authors conclude that both strategy paths can be followed to reach a positive turnaround outcome.

Morrow et al. (2004) support the general assertion of Pearce and Robbins that retrenchment builds the basis of a successful turnaround. They nonetheless insist that the turnaround strategy has to fit the firm's competitive environment. More explicitly, growth industries are more likely to apply asset retrenchment instead of cost retrenchment, since they need to invest in their development due to the competitive environment (Morrow et al. 2004).

An early contribution propagating a holistic approach towards turnaround management, represented in Figure 3, comes to us through the work of Krueger and Willard (1991). A considerable distinction to previously mentioned models is their emphasis on relativizing a firm's condition to benchmarks like industry or competitors' key performance indicators (KPIs).

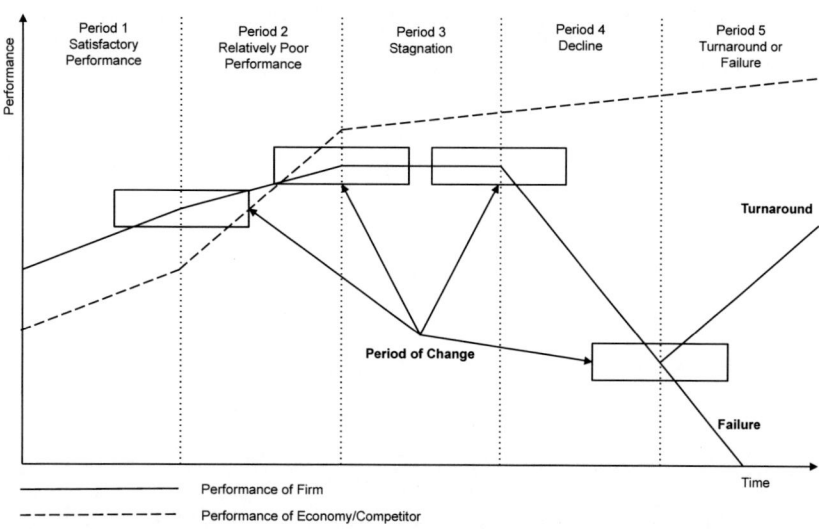

Figure 3: Turnaround lifecycle (adapted from Krueger and Willard 1991)

The need for strategic change of an organization is dependent on the cause of decline, which presets the strategic course of actions. According to Barker III. & Duhaime (1997), firm-based declines have a higher urgency to change strategy whereas external causes of steep performance, e.g. due to economic recession, lead to a lower involvement of strategy change. Figure 4 captures the different influencing factors for strategic change.

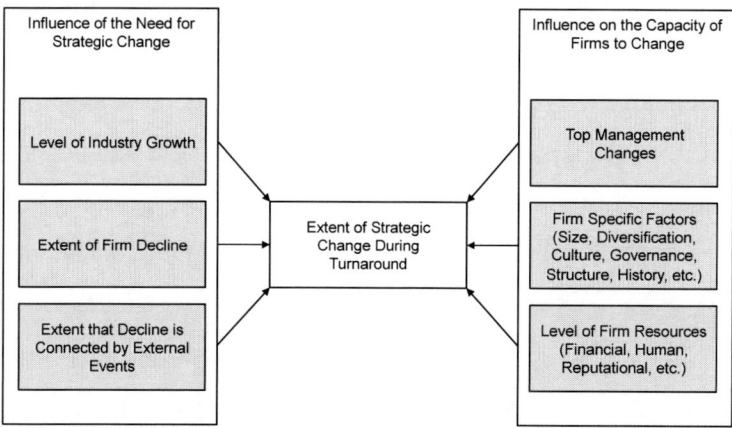

Figure 4: Model of Proposed Factors Influencing the Level of Strategic Change (Barker III. and Duhaime 1997)

Hofer's (1980) contribution to the turnaround strategy debate is based on a situational approach. Organizations operating almost at break-even tend to pursue retrenchment/cost-cutting strategies and organizations operating far below break-even tend to pursue asset-reduction and revenue-increasing strategies. These findings can be clustered with those of Hambrick and Schecter (1983) who also pursue a situational approach. According to them, one out of three major turnaround strategies ("asset/cost surgery, selective product/market pruning, piecemeal strategy", p. 247) is chosen depending on capacity utilization (low: asset/cost surgery; high: selective product/market pruning) and market share (high: piecemeal strategy).

The ongoing discussions of turnaround recipes show the complexity and challenging nature of successful turnarounds. A more recent contribution to this debate is a *"shifting balance perspective"* (Schmitt and Raisch, 2010) that supports neither a stand-alone retrenchment approach nor a simultaneous approach of retrenchment and strategic recovery. Instead it supports balancing retrenchment and growth strategies throughout the turnaround process.

Little research was dedicated to other strategies than retrenchment, however Chowdhury and Lang (1996) considered growth strategies as an alternative to retrenchment. This view is supported by Rasheed (2005), who, based on a study of small businesses, claims that growth strategies are advisable in case of sufficient resources. As part of a growth strategy, Morrow et al. (2007) suggest growth through a recombination of existing resources. This strategic focus was identified to be particularly effective for creating shareholder value, subject to the condition that the recombination activities must be difficult to imitate for competitors.

Other perspectives on turnaround strategies propose a more situational approach: the strategy has to be aligned with the cause of decline, being classified as either strategic or operational (Schendel et al. 1976). Accordingly, declines caused by strategic factors would be tackled by strategic moves, whereas declines caused by operational factors would be tackled by operational moves. If poorly managed, namely a non-fitting strategy has been chosen, the turnaround would fail – explaining the reason for failing turnarounds by a misleading strategy (Schendel et al.

1976, Schendel & Patton 1976, Hofer & Schendel, 1978, Hofer 1980). Hofer (1980) classifies the turnaround itself as "strategic" or "operational" and comes to the same conclusions regarding the fit as Schendel.

3.2 Extensive Model of Organizational Decline and Turnaround

Referring back to the two-stage model of Pearce and Robbins (1992), recent research proposes a more complex and dynamic turnaround process model (Trahms et al. 2013). The proposal, which is summarized in Figure 5, is an attempt to synthesize existing cresearch and will be examined more closely.

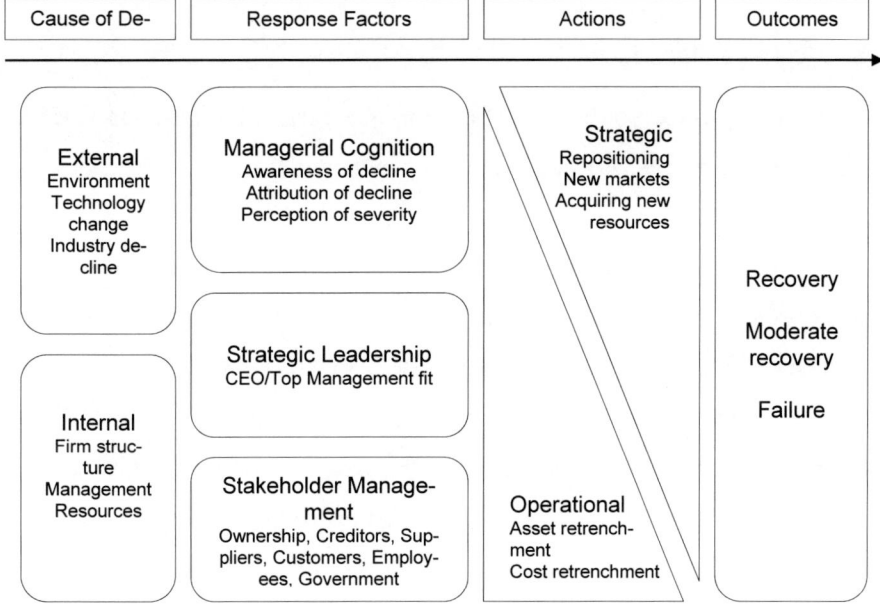

Figure 5: Classification of triggering factors (adapted from Trahms et al. 2013)

As for the cause of decline, the model is in accordance with the findings of Pearce and Robbin's model: one can distinguish between external and internal causes of decline (Cameron et al. 1988, Arogyaswamy, Barker and Yasai-Ardekani 1995). The heart of the model deals with the response to decline and is further specified.

3.2.1 Managerial Cognition

Effective decision-making by top management is dependent on the thorough examination and analysis of the environment (Morrow et al. 2007). The top management must be able to detect the source of decline and at the same time understand how the dysfunctional source affects the organization in order to undertake respective actions (Barker III. 2005). Barker revealed within his study that this process is influenced by the subjective perception of executive managers. Musteen, Liang and Barker (2011) reinforce this view by stating that the perception of decline severity is influenced by the manager's age, level of experience and functional background. To overcome unconscious biases, Barker (2005) proposes greater diversity in the executive board, outside advisors, as well as a direct interaction with stakeholders and employees instead of relying on filtered data.

3.2.2 Strategic Leadership

Strategic Leadership refers to the role of the top management in a turnaround process. Arogyaswamy et al. (1995) detected poor managerial quality as a root cause of organizational decline. A change in top management right at the beginning of a turnaround situation may be seen as an ultimate sign of determination for turning around a declining performance, in order to regain the trust and support of stockholders (Chen 2008). However, the effectiveness of and contribution to performance recovery of this strategic action is dependent on the cause of decline. Simply changing top management has provided no evidence of improving a turnaround situation (Chen 2008). Instead, organizations suffering from economic decline may need the experience of the CEO to lead through the turnaround – thus a replacement could have a negative effect (Arogyaswamy et al. 1995). On the other hand, if the cause of the decline is firm-based and thus the need for strategic turnaround is higher, executive managers often block necessary actions due to self-esteem reasons: confessing mismanagement and pointing to internal causes of decline can naturally be accompanied with a negative image of the top management. Under such preconditions, firm-based declines could be recovered easier by a change in top management (Barker III. and Patterson 1996, Barker III. and Duhaime 1997, Barker III. and Patterson 2001). Chen (2008) adds here that the effectiveness of a CEO replacement increases along with the degree of misfit of the predecessor

CEO. Additionally, longer-tenured CEOs may be less effective in turnaround contexts (Chen and Hambrick 2012). Overall, the literature shows that there are controversial views on top management replacement. Charmeli and Schaubroeck (2006) found that thorough behavioral integration of the top management team affects the perception of quality of strategic actions and positively influences the turnaround process.

3.2.3 Stakeholder Management

Increasing efficiency is an integral part of the turnaround as it stops further decline and helps regain shareholders' trust and support (Arogyaswamy and Yasai-Ardekani 1997). When it comes to the actual response of a decline, management has the choice between operational and strategic actions or applies a mix of both activities.

3.2.4 Strategic activities

Strategic activities comprise acquiring and repositioning strategies. Retrenchment of assets and costs are defined as operational activities. The controversial debate on the applicability of retrenchment as well as of strategic activities was discussed earlier above (please refer to section 3.1).

3.2.5 Turnaround Outcomes

Boyne (2006) described three potential outcomes of turnarounds. The most favorable outcome obviously will be a successful turnaround. Another possibility is a continuing poor performance of an organization although turnaround strategies are applied. Depending on the management's motivation of turning around, the turnaround process will be repeated until the operation turns out to be successful. Poorly managed turnaround situations and false strategy application may lead to the third possible outcome, which is a terminal decline. Likewise, Moulton and Thomas (1996) identified bankruptcy and partial turnarounds, e.g. through acquisition by another firm, as possible turnaround outcomes.

Besides the types of outcomes, the question of what constitutes a successful outcome is also addressed in the literature. Barker and Duhaime (1997) define turnaround success to be reached if KPIs are positive above the risk-free rate of return. These measures should stay stable or improve for more than one, respectively three years (no consensus to be found in literature) to classify the turnaround as being successful (Morrow et al. 2007 Barker & Duhaime 1997, Bruton et al. 2003).

4 Research Gaps

The first step of turnaround management is to detect the actual need for a turnaround, to create awareness and understand the cause(s) of decline. Within this field of research there is still a need to examine the practices of top management – not only within the first stage of the process but throughout the entire turnaround process (Lohrke 2004). Further research should be conducted in the field of turnaround strategies for small family businesses, focusing on how the characteristics of such businesses affect turnaround management (Cater & Schwab 2008). Boyne (2006) identified a turnaround model for public organizations derived from existing literature on private-sector turnarounds. The exact combination of strategies and the conditions under which they work are areas for further research in the public sector of declining institutions. Another gap for public institutions is to examine the political relationships between the organization and auditors, professional associations and government agencies (Boyne & Meier 2009). Finally, when Hambrick and D'Aveni (1988) explained the process of decline they pointed to the need of further research regarding the psychological and sociological mechanisms, which catch large organizations in downward spirals.

5 Summary and Conclusion

The existing literature shows that there is no single framework or "one size fits all" approach for turnaround situations. The main research results were created from 1975 to 2000; more recent studies use these findings as basis for controversial discussions but no additional research streams could be identified. Great efforts have been put into identifying the influencing factors for the strategic fit of turnaround actions. To sum up the main findings, turnaround management refers to the recovery of a decline (Pears & Robbins 1993), the causes of which can be split into external and internal drivers (Schendel et al. 1976, Schendel & Patton 1975/76, Hofer & Schendel, 1978, Hofer 1980, Cameron et al. 1988, Arogyaswamy, Barker & Yasai-Ardekani 1995). Turnaround strategies comprise retrenchment and growth. The controversial debate on strategic fit has not yet reached a conclusion. However the shifting balance perspective of Schmitt and Raisch (2010) proposes a solution that could serve as a reasonable compromise. Top management replacement is one of the turnaround activities that have gained considerable attention in academic literature. Because turnaround situations depend on manifold factors like industry, company size, market position et cetera, it is not surprising that no consensus has been reached on the issue of top management replacement either.

To conclude, turnaround management is highly sensitive to environmental conditions and requires further research to shed light on this complex but yet crucial topic for declining organizations.

References

Arogyaswamy, K., Barker, V., & Yasai-Ardekani, M. 1995. Firm turnarounds: An integrative two-stage model. *Journal of Management Studies*, 32, pp. 493-525.

Arogyaswamy, K. & Yasai-Ardekani, M. 1997. Organizational turnaround: Understanding the role of cutbacks, efficiency improvements, and investment in technology. Engineering Management, *IEEE Transactions on*, 44 (1), pp. 3--11.

Arpi, B. (1999). *International Turnaround Management – From Crisis to Revival and Long-Term Profitability*. Palgrave Macmillan UK, p. 4

Barker III, V. L. 2005. Traps in diagnosing organization failure. *Journal of Business Strategy*, 26 (2), pp. 44--50.

BARKER III, V. L. & Duhaime, I. M. 1997. Strategic change in the turnaround process: theory and empirical evidence. *Strategic management journal*, 18 (1), pp. 13--38.

Barker III, V. L., Patterson Jr, P. W. & Mueller, G. C. 2001. Organizational causes and strategic consequences of the extent of top management team replacement during turnaround attempts. *Journal of Management Studies*, 38 (2), pp. 235-270.

Barker, V. L. & Mone, M. A. 1994. Retrenchment: cause of turnaround or consequence of decline?. *Strategic management journal*, 15 (5), pp. 395-405.

Barker, V. L. & Patterson, P. W. 1996. Top management team tenure and top manager causal attributions at declining firms attempting turnarounds. *Group & Organization Management*, 21 (3), pp. 304-336.

Boyne, G. A. 2006. Strategies for Public Service Turnaround Lessons from the Private Sector. *Administration & Society*, 38 (3), pp. 365-388.

Boyne, G. A. and Meier, K. J. 2009. Environmental change, human resources and organizational turnaround. *Journal of Management Studies*, 46 (5), pp. 835-863.

Bruton, G. D., Ahlstrom, D., & Wan, J. C. 2003. Turnaround in East Asian firms: Evidence from ethnic overseas Chinese communities. *Strategic Management Journal*, 24: 519-540.

Cameron, K. S., Kim, M. U. & Whetten, D. A. 1987. Organizational effects of decline and turbulence. Administrative Science Quarterly, pp. 222--240.

Cameron, K. S., Sutton, R. I., & Whetten, D. A. (Eds.). 1988. *Readings in organizational decline: Frameworks, research, and prescriptions*. Cambridge, MA: Ballinger.

Carmeli, A. & Schaubroeck, J. 2006. Top management team behavioral integration, decision quality, and organizational decline. *The Leadership Quarterly*, 17 (5), pp. 441-453.

Cater, J. & Schwab, A. 2008. Turnaround strategies in established small family firms. *Family Business Review*, 21 (1), pp. 31-50.

Chen, G. 2008. Performance Consequences of CEO Replacement in Turnaround Situations. *Academy of Management Annual Meeting Proceedings*, 2008, p1-6, 6p. Publisher: Academy of Management.

Chen, G., & Hambrick, D. C. 2012. CEO replacement in turnaround situations: Executive (mis)fit and its performance implications. *Organization Science*, 23: 225-243.

Chowdhury S.D. and Lang J. R. 1996. Turnaround In Small Firms: An Assessment Of Efficiency Strategies, *Journal of Business Research*, Vol.36, No.2, pp.169-179.

D'aveni, R. A. 1989. The aftermath of organizational decline: A longitudinal study of the strategic and managerial characteristics of declining firms. *Academy of Management Journal*, 32 (3), pp. 577--605.

Hambrick, D.C. 1985. Turnaround strategies. In W. Guth (Ed.), *Handbook of business strategy* (pp. 3-32). Boston: Warren, Gorham and Lamont.

Hambrick, D. C. & D'aveni, R. A. 1988. Large corporate failures as downward spirals. *Administrative Science Quarterly*, pp. 1--23.

Hambrick, D. C. & Schecter, S. M. 1983. Turnaround strategies for mature industrial-product business units. *Academy of Management Journal*, 26 (2), pp. 231--248.

Hofer, C. W. 1980. Turnaround strategies. *Journal of Business Strategy*, 1 (1), pp. 19--31.

Hofer, C.W. & Schendel, D. 1978. *Strategy Formulation: Analytical Concepts*, West Publishing, St Paul, MN.

Khandwalla Pradip, N. 1992. *Innovative Corporate Turnaround*, Sage Publications, New Delhi.

Krueger, D. A., & Willard, G. E. 1991. Turnarounds: A process, not an event. *Academy of Management Best Papers Proceedings*, pp. 26-30.

Lohrke, F. T., Bedeian, A. G. & Palmer, T. B. 2004. The role of top management teams in formulating and implementing turnaround strategies: a review and research agenda. *International Journal of Management Reviews*, 5 (2), pp. 63--90.

Morrow, J., Johnson, R. A. & Busenitz, L. W. 2004. The effects of cost and asset retrenchment on firm performance: the overlooked role of a firm's competitive environment. *Journal of Management*, 30 (2), pp. 189--208.

Morrow, J. L., Sirmon, D. G., Hitt, M. A., & Holcomb, T. R. 2007. Creating value in the face of declining performance: Firm strategies and organizational recovery. *Strategic Management Journal*, 28: 271-283.

Moulton, W. N. & Thomas, H. 1996. Business Failure Pathways: Environmental Stress and Organizational Response. *Journal of Management*, 22 (4), pp. 571-595.

Musteen, M., Liang, X. & Barker III, V. L. 2011. Personality, perceptions and retrenchment decisions of managers in response to decline: Evidence from a decision-making study. *The Leadership Quarterly*, 22 (5), pp. 926--941.

Pearce II, J. A. & Robbins, K. 1993. Toward improved theory and research on business turnaround. *Journal of Management*, 19 (3), pp. 613--636.

Rasheed, H. S. 2005. Turnaround strategies for declining small business: the effects of performance and resources. *Journal of Developmental Entrepreneurship*, 10 (03), pp. 239--252.

Robbins, D. K. and Pearce, J. A. 1992. Turnaround: Retrenchment and recovery. *Strategic Management Journal*, 13 (4), pp. 287--309.

Schendel, D. and Patton, G. 1975. An empirical study of corporate stagnation and trunaraound. *Academy of Management Proceedings,* 1975 (1), pp. 49--51.

Schendel, D. & G. R. Patton 1976. 'Corporate Stagnation and Turnaround', *Journal of Economics and Business*, 28(3), Spring-Summer, pp. 236–241.

Schendel, D. E., Patton, G. R., & Riggs, J. 1976. Corporate turnaround strategies: A study of profit decline and recovery. *Journal of General Management*, 3: 3-12.

Schmitt, A. & Raisch, S. 2010. *Neither black nor white yet: the shifting balance between retrenchment and recovery in corporate turnarounds*. 2010 (1), pp. 1-6.

Trahms, C. A., Ndofor, H. A. & Sirmon, D. G. 2013. Organizational Decline and Turnaround A Review and Agenda for Future Research. *Journal of Management*, 39 (5), pp. 1277--1307.

***ibidem*-**Verlag

Melchiorstr. 15

D-70439 Stuttgart

info@ibidem-verlag.de

www.ibidem-verlag.de
www.ibidem.eu
www.edition-noema.de
www.autorenbetreuung.de